Contents

Basic Tools

1

Getting started

Photoshop Elements 2.0 is the little brother of the art and design industry standard Adobe Photoshop. It is a powerful art package which you can use to paint, write text, retouch photos and make images ready for the web. After only a few lessons you will be creating amazing pictures and effects.

Let's get started!

○   Load Adobe Photoshop Elements 2.0. You can do this in one of two ways:

○   *Either* double-click the Elements icon

○   *or* click Start at the bottom left of the screen, then click Programs. When the programs pop up, click:

The Opening Screen

> Your screen will look like the one below:

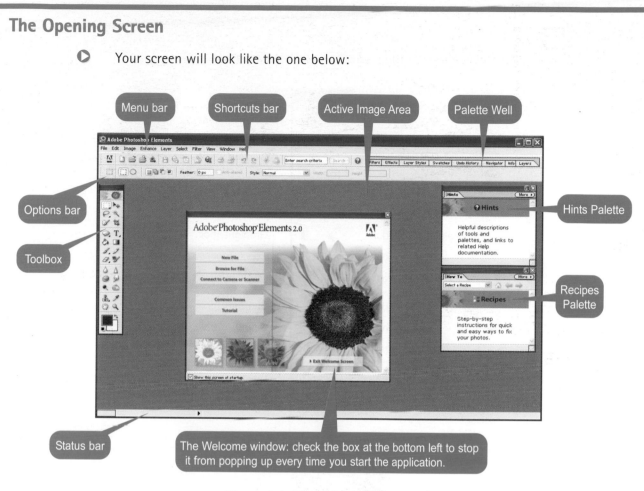

Figure 1.1: The Opening Screen

Menu bar The Menu bar contains menus organised by topic. The Help option on this menu is useful for getting extra information on a particular topic.

Shortcuts bar Just below the Menu bar at the top of the screen is the Shortcuts bar. This has icons that may be clicked instead of choosing common options from the Menu bar.

Options bar This bar changes to give you relevant options for whichever tool you have chosen.

Palette well This is a great feature that keeps your palettes stored tidily ready to use. When you click a tab, the palette will appear.

Toolbox Down the left side of the screen is the Toolbox. This is where you will choose the tools to create or retouch your pictures.

Tip: The **Shortcuts bar** must be present in order to use the **Palette Well**. Select **Window, Shortcuts** from the **Menu bar** to display it if it is not open.

The Toolbox

The Toolbox holds all the editing, selection and drawing tools.

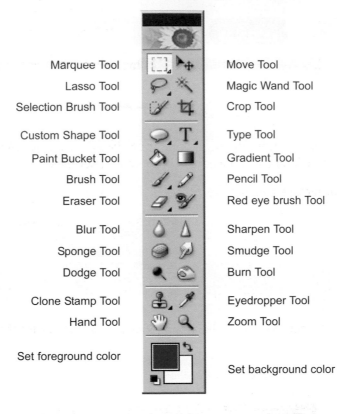

Marquee Tool	Move Tool
Lasso Tool	Magic Wand Tool
Selection Brush Tool	Crop Tool
Custom Shape Tool	Type Tool
Paint Bucket Tool	Gradient Tool
Brush Tool	Pencil Tool
Eraser Tool	Red eye brush Tool
Blur Tool	Sharpen Tool
Sponge Tool	Smudge Tool
Dodge Tool	Burn Tool
Clone Stamp Tool	Eyedropper Tool
Hand Tool	Zoom Tool
Set foreground color	Set background color

Figure 1.2

Try clicking the tools; you will notice the Options bar above the Toolbox changes to give options for that particular tool.

You must select a tool in order to use it. The currently selected tool will be highlighted. Some of the tools have a small black triangle at the bottom right corner of the icon, showing that there are additional tools behind them. You can hold down the left mouse button or right-click on a tool icon to display the hidden tools. Then click the tool you want to select.

Creating a new image

If the Welcome Screen is still showing (the one with the Photoshop sunflower logo) follow these steps to close it.

- ▶ First make sure the checkbox at the bottom left of the screen is deselected (click it once to remove the green tick), so that the Welcome Screen doesn't appear next time you open Photoshop.

- ▶ Click OK in the dialogue box that appears.

Adobe Photoshop Elements ☒

⚠ You can show the <u>Welcome</u> screen again by selecting
'Welcome' from the Window menu.

OK

▶ Click the Exit Welcome Screen button in the bottom right of the Welcome Screen.

▶ Exit Welcome Screen

▶ Choose File, New from the Menu bar, or on the Shortcuts bar click the New icon. The New Image window will appear showing default settings.

▶ Give your picture a name: Brush Test.

▶ Set the Width to 1000 pixels, the Height to 750 pixels and the Resolution to 72 pixels/inch.

Tip: 72 dpi (dots per inch) is the norm for most computer screens, but if you need to print something it may need to be a higher resolution.

▶ Set the Contents to White. This is the most suitable colour for the image you are going to create.

▶ The Mode should be set to RGB Colour.

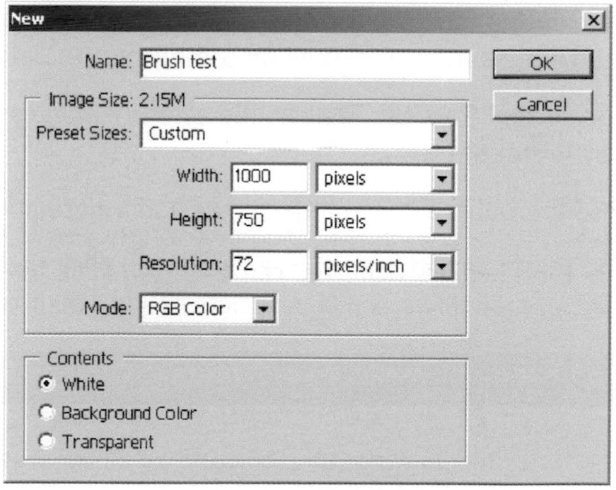

New ☒

Name: Brush test   OK

Image Size: 2.15M   Cancel

Preset Sizes: Custom ▼

Width: 1000   pixels ▼

Height: 750   pixels ▼

Resolution: 72   pixels/inch ▼

Mode: RGB Color ▼

Contents
⦿ White
○ Background Color
○ Transparent

Figure 1.3: New Image settings

Tip: Make sure you have selected **pixels** and **pixels/inch** in the drop-down lists. Photoshop may initially assume **cm** and **pixels/cm**.

▶ Click OK.

Your screen will look like this:

Figure 1.4: Blank canvas

The Brush Tool

The Brush Tool is a painting tool. The width of the brush, the amount and density of the paint on the brush, and how it behaves all depend on settings in the Options bar.

> Select the Brush Tool from the Toolbox. (Be careful – it is easy to select the Selection Brush Tool by mistake.)

We now need to use the Options bar to pick colours and other options.

> In the Brush Presets drop-down list (see Figure 1.5) click the down-arrow to display default brushes. Scroll down and choose Soft Round 100 pixels.

Tip: If the **Options bar** is not visible, select **Window**, **Options** from the **Menu bar**.

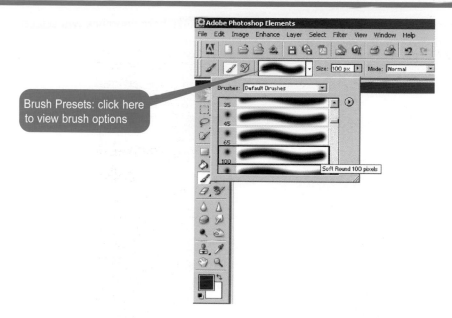

Brush Presets: click here to view brush options

Figure 1.5: Choosing a brush

◉ Further to the right on the Options bar, you will notice the Size option has changed to match the brush you have chosen. If you want a different brush size, click on the arrow and change the brush size to exactly the size you want.

◉ The next option is Mode – leave this set to Normal.

◉ Next to that is the Opacity option slider. You can use the slider to increase/decrease opacity or you can simply type in the opacity you want.

Note: Reducing opacity is like adding water to your paintbrush – some of the background shows through.

◉ Next, select a colour to paint with by clicking the Set Foreground Color icon at the bottom of the Toolbox.

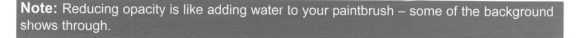

Set Foreground Color   Set Background Color

You need to imagine that the foreground colour is the wet paint on your brush and the background colour is the colour you would find if you wiped the paint away.

◉ Click on the foreground colour square and the Color Picker will pop up. The central slider allows you to choose any colour in the colour spectrum: as you slide it, the left-hand box changes.

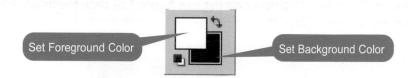

Tip: You can swap foreground and background colours in the two swatches by clicking the two-headed arrow between them.

▶ Choose a bright blue and then left-click in the left box. Anywhere you click will select that shade and you can choose to saturate the colour from 0% to 100% and from white to black.

▶ Click OK.

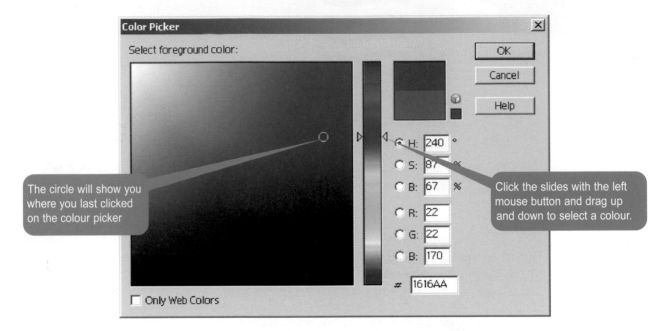

The circle will show you where you last clicked on the colour picker

Click the slides with the left mouse button and drag up and down to select a colour.

Figure 1.6: Choosing a colour

▶ Now left-click on the white canvas to paint a blue blob.

▶ Try different brush sizes and brush styles; change the opacity and get used to choosing new colours to see what happens. Write your name and generally have a play.

> **Tip:** All these effects are created by selecting different brushes and either painting or simply clicking on the canvas with different colours.
>
> The more interesting brush shapes are near the bottom of the Brush Presets drop-down list, so make sure you scroll all the way down!

Figure 1.7

Zoom Options

The Title bar says Brush test @ 100%(RGB) which means the canvas is at its best viewable setting. However, there are times when you need to zoom in or out.

> **Tip:** Don't worry if your Title bar says a different percentage – this just means you've been viewing the image at a different size.

▶ Click the Zoom Tool in the Toolbox.

▶ In the Options bar, select the Zoom In option.

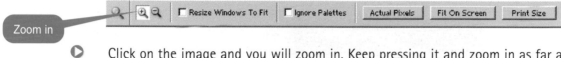

▶ Click on the image and you will zoom in. Keep pressing it and zoom in as far as it will go.

Figure 1.8

The squares that make up a picture are called pixels. When you created this canvas, you specified that it should be 1000 pixels wide and 750 pixels high.

▶ Now zoom out, either by using the Zoom Out icon or by clicking the Fit on Screen button in the Options bar.

▶ Select File, Close from the Menu bar – there is no need to save this so click No when prompted to save.

A Starry night

◉ Make a new canvas 600 pixels wide and 400 high, 72 pixels/inch, RGB with a white background, and click OK.

> **Note:** If you don't enter a name for the image here, the image will automatically be called something like **Untitled-1**. Once you save the document under a chosen file name, the image name will become the file name.

A really good tip when working on a picture is to click the Maximise icon in the top right of your canvas. This gives you a neutral border to paint across and also when you zoom in, it shows you the maximum amount of picture on-screen.

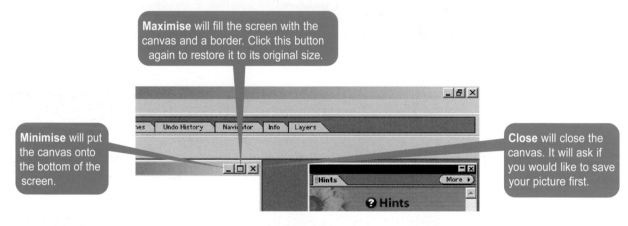

Figure 1.9

◉ Choose a big soft brush, size 500 pixels, and set Opacity to 50%.

◉ Spray the background very dark blue with a soft blue gradient coming from the bottom; use Figure 1.11 as a guide.

Undoing mistakes

 If you don't like the last stroke you painted, you can undo it by clicking the Step Backward icon.

You can undo a whole lot of strokes using Window, Undo History, or by clicking the Undo History tab in the Palette Well.

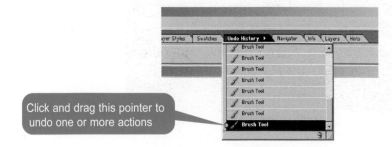

Figure 1.10: The Undo History Palette

You cannot undo just action number 3, for example. You must undo every action back to that action.

 You can redo the actions by clicking the **Step Forward** icon on the **Shortcuts bar**.

> **Note:** You can use the shortcut key combination **Ctrl-Z** to undo the last action.

▶ Undo some or all of the strokes you have made and click the **Step Forward** icon to bring them back.

▶ Now pick a hard-edged brush around 60 pixels in size and select a white foreground. Change the opacity to 100%.

▶ Spray a moon high up on your canvas.

▶ Pick another soft brush and set the pixels to 120, with opacity 10%.

▶ Spray a little glow over the moon.

> **Tip:** If your moon looks grey instead of white it is probably because the **Opacity** is less than **100%**. Change this in the **Options bar** if you need to.

▶ Now the fun part! Choose the Star brush, start with 70 pixels and spray stars of varying sizes and brightness in your night sky, by clicking on the canvas. Add a glow to some of them.

> **Tip:** The **Star** brushes don't look much like stars in the Brush Presets drop-down list. Scroll about two thirds of the way down the list. If you hover the cursor over a brush the name of the brush will appear.

▶ The finishing touch is to add the trees. Choose the Scattered Maple Leaves brush, set the opacity to 75, pick a blue-black colour and add trees and bushes. Try to give your picture depth by using small leaves in the distance and large ones in the foreground.

Figure 1.11: A starry night

▶ That's it!

Now we'll save and close the image:

▶ On the Menu bar click File, Save As. In the File name box type Starry night and ensure the format is on the setting Photoshop. Use the navigation options at the top of the Save As dialogue box to select where you want the file to be saved.

▶ Click Save.

 ▶ Close the image by clicking the small cross in the top right of the image window. Be careful to select the cross that belongs to the image, not the one above it which will close Photoshop.

A greyscale drawing

In Photoshop there is a huge library of brushes. You can create great-looking artwork in a very short time just by using different brushes, colours and opacity. You can try out different brushes to create your own greyscale masterpiece similar to Figure 1.12.

Figure 1.12

▶ Open a new canvas, width 400, height 200, mode greyscale with a white background. Unless specified otherwise, just leave the resolution as 72 pixels/inch for future images.

▶ Choose a large brush set to 100% opacity and paint the canvas black.

▶ Change the foreground colour to white.

▶ In the Brush Presets drop-down list you can change the Default Brushes list. Click on the Default Brushes menu and choose Wet Media Brushes, which will give a great 'painterly' effect.

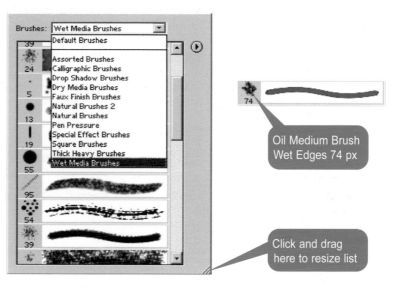

Figure 1.13

▶ Choose the Oil Medium Brush Wet Edges 74 px, and reduce its opacity to 30 pixels.

▶ Use different layers of paint to build up foggy mountains and clouds.

▶ Set your brushes back to the Default Brushes.

▶ Use the Grass or Dune Grass brush to paint in the grass. Remember to use a larger brush in the foreground. You can click Ctrl-Z to undo anything you don't like!

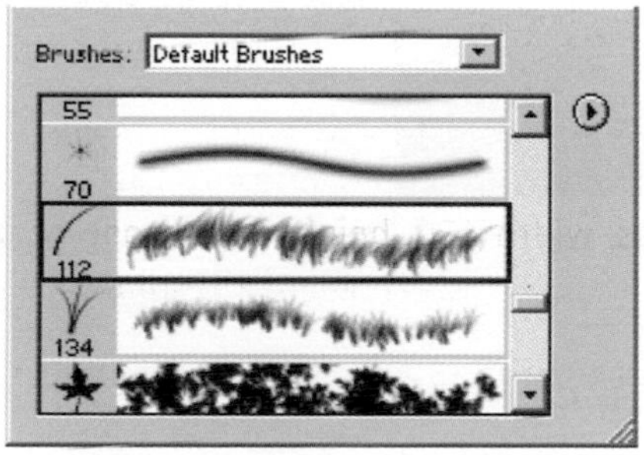

Figure 1.14: The Dune Grass brush

▶ Save your picture as Stormy Mountain.

Printing

◑   From the Menu bar select File, Page Setup.

◑   Choose your printer's Paper Size and set the Orientation of the picture to Landscape. Click OK.

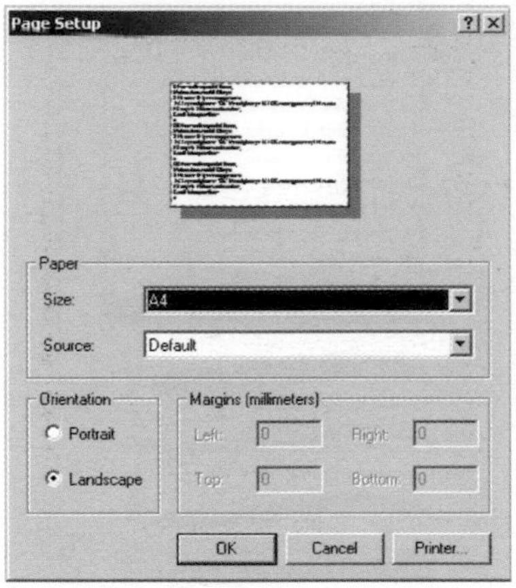

Figure 1.15: The Page Setup dialogue box

Before you print, it is wise to select Print Preview so that you know what the printout will look like.

◑   From the File menu select Print Preview. The dialogue box appears.

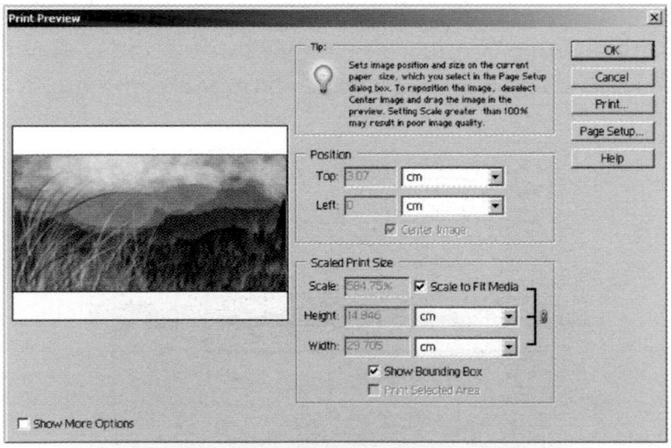

Figure 1.16: The Print Preview dialogue box

◑   Select Scale to Fit Media.

◑   Click the Print button to print, or just click OK to close Print Preview without printing.

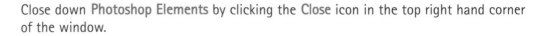 ◑   Select File, Close or click the Close icon in the top right hand corner of the canvas to close the picture. Click Yes if prompted to save changes.

◑   Close down Photoshop Elements by clicking the Close icon in the top right hand corner of the window.

Image modes

So far we have touched on RGB mode and Grayscale mode. There are a few more that you might come across so here's a quick guide to all of the modes in Photoshop Elements.

RGB mode

This is the default mode for Photoshop images. RGB uses three colours (also called channels) to reproduce over 16 million colours.

In RGB mode this image is 283K

Indexed Color mode

This mode uses up to 256 colours. If you convert an RGB file to an Indexed file, the file size will decrease but the image quality will also be reduced. Because it has fewer colours, it has to approximate some of the RGB colours. GIF files use Indexed Color.

In Indexed Color mode this image is 94K

Grayscale mode

Grayscale uses up to 256 shades of grey. If you scan an image in black and white it will probably be displayed in Grayscale mode.

In **Grayscale mode** this image is **94K**

Bitmap mode

Bitmap mode assigns one of two colours (black or white) to each pixel in an image. This results in very small file sizes but unless your image is black and white it will be severely degraded if you save it as a Bitmap.

In **Bitmap mode** this image is **12K**

Changing image modes

Whenever you convert a file to a worse-quality mode (for example from RGB to Indexed Color) you should always save a backup in the original mode. You should also aim to do as much editing as possible in the better colour mode before converting.

To convert an image to a different mode:

▶   Select Image, Mode from the Menu bar, then select a mode from the list. If a mode is greyed-out in the menu, it means it is not available for the current image.

Selections

Making selections

A selection masks off an area so that you can paint it, move it, copy it or fill it with special effects, without affecting the rest of the image.

There are four basic tools for making selections:

 The Marquee Tool (Rectangular or Ellipse)

 The Lasso Tool

 The Magic Wand Tool

 The Selection Brush Tool

The Marquee Tool

The Marquee Tool enables you to make selections using either a rectangle or an ellipse. We'll try them out now.

 ◗ Click on the Set Background Color icon and change it to white.

◗ Open a new canvas with dimensions 500 x 500 pixels, resolution 72 pixels/inch, mode RGB colour, contents background color.

 ◗ Click the Maximize icon to centralize your canvas.

 ◗ Click the Rectangular Marquee Tool in the Toolbox.

The Options bar for the Marquee Tool will probably already be visible. If it is not, click Window on the Menu bar then click Options.

Drawing with the Marquee Tool

▶   Set your options to match Figure 2.1.

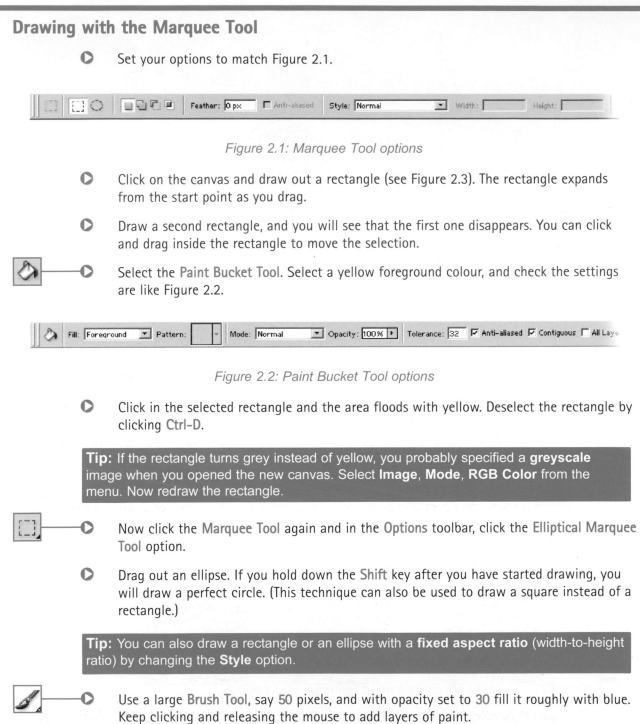

Figure 2.1: Marquee Tool options

▶   Click on the canvas and draw out a rectangle (see Figure 2.3). The rectangle expands from the start point as you drag.

▶   Draw a second rectangle, and you will see that the first one disappears. You can click and drag inside the rectangle to move the selection.

▶   Select the Paint Bucket Tool. Select a yellow foreground colour, and check the settings are like Figure 2.2.

Figure 2.2: Paint Bucket Tool options

▶   Click in the selected rectangle and the area floods with yellow. Deselect the rectangle by clicking Ctrl-D.

> **Tip:** If the rectangle turns grey instead of yellow, you probably specified a **greyscale** image when you opened the new canvas. Select **Image**, **Mode**, **RGB Color** from the menu. Now redraw the rectangle.

▶   Now click the Marquee Tool again and in the Options toolbar, click the Elliptical Marquee Tool option.

▶   Drag out an ellipse. If you hold down the Shift key after you have started drawing, you will draw a perfect circle. (This technique can also be used to draw a square instead of a rectangle.)

> **Tip:** You can also draw a rectangle or an ellipse with a **fixed aspect ratio** (width-to-height ratio) by changing the **Style** option.

▶   Use a large Brush Tool, say 50 pixels, and with opacity set to 30 fill it roughly with blue. Keep clicking and releasing the mouse to add layers of paint.

Figure 2.3: Selecting and filling shapes

Moving a selection

Your blue circle should still be selected.

○ Change the background colour to black.

○ From the Toolbox select the Move Tool.

○ You will notice that a box has appeared around your selected circle. Click and drag inside the circle to move it over the square.

The little boxes around the edge of the box are called nodes. See what happens when you place the cursor over the nodes: the arrows show you which direction you can stretch, resize or even rotate the circle.

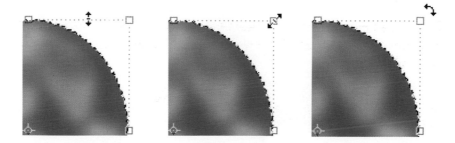

You must complete the transformation (i.e. the stretching or rotation of the selection) in one of three ways:

○ *Either* press Enter, *or* double-click inside the transformation box, *or* click the Commit Transform icon in the Options bar.

You will notice that you can see the black background colour where the circle was. This needs to be remedied.

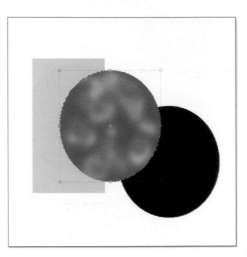

Figure 2.4: Moving shapes

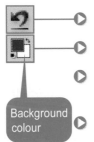

Undo the move by clicking the **Step Backward** icon or by pressing **Ctrl-Z**.

Change the background colour to white, and then repeat the move.

Have a play with it, and leave it overlapping the yellow square. Complete the resizing (**transformation** in Photoshop terminology) by pressing **Enter**.

From the **Select** menu choose **Deselect**, or press **Ctrl-D**.

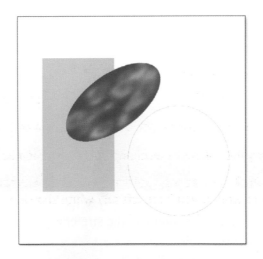

Figure 2.5: A white background is left where the ellipse was

Tip: You may notice that there is a trace of blue left around where the circle was. If you have this, use a small paintbrush with **100%** opacity to paint over it in white.

The Magic Wand Tool

Using the Magic Wand Tool you can select an area of a particular colour. You can set the Tolerance level so that colours which are almost but not quite the same will also be selected.

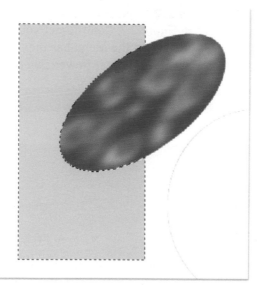

> Click the Magic Wand Tool and then click in the yellow rectangle.

The portion of the rectangle not overlapped by the circle will be selected.

Figure 2.6: Selecting with the Magic Wand Tool

Setting the Tolerance level

Now we will experiment with setting the Tolerance level of the Magic Wand Tool.

> In the Tool Options for the Magic Wand, set the Tolerance level to 0.

> Click in the blue circle. Probably only a small portion of it will be selected.

> Keep increasing the Tolerance level and clicking in the circle.

When you have set the Tolerance level sufficiently high, the whole ellipse will be selected when you click in it. It won't work if you have left any white showing when you painted in the circle.

Adding and subtracting selections

Now suppose you wanted to select the rectangle in addition to the ellipse already selected. You add to selections by keeping the Shift key pressed while you make another selection.

> You can close this image without saving – that's enough practice!

The Lasso Tool

We will put some of our new skills to test to draw a pattern of flowers using the Selection and Brush tools.

▶   Change the background colour to green.

▶   Open a new canvas, and specify a 500 x 500 canvas, RGB Color and Background Color as Contents.

▶   Select the Lasso Tool and then place your cursor on the canvas. By dragging the cursor, draw a flower shape as in Figure 2.7. Don't forget you can have as many goes as you like to get it right. Just click Select on the Menu bar then click on Deselect. This will deselect the flower so you can now draw another flower shape.

Tip: You can use the shortcut **Ctrl-D** to deselect.

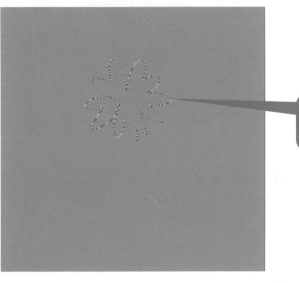

The outline of black and white moving dashes is called the marquee.

Figure 2.7: Flower selection

Tip: Don't worry if you draw a wobbly line or spray the wrong colour, just undo using **Ctrl-Z** and try again. Practice makes perfect!

▶   Now select the Paint Bucket Tool. Choose a white foreground colour. Move the cursor over to the canvas, click and colour in the petals.

▶   On the Select menu click Deselect or use the shortcut Ctrl-D. You can now draw the next part of your picture.

In the Toolbox click on the Marquee Tool. In the Options bar select the Elliptical Marquee Tool. Draw a circle in the middle of the flower. You can use the arrow keys on the keyboard to nudge the selection into the perfect position, or you can drag the circle.

Click the Brush Tool and paint yellow in the circle selection. Deselect when you have finished coloring.

Figure 2.8: Flower

Hopefully you will have a flower like this! Now we are going to select the daisy and duplicate it all over the canvas.

Pasting daisies

Click the Magic Wand Tool and select the yellow center.

Keep Shift held down while you click in the white part of the flower to select it. You may have to click in several petals if your yellow circle overlaps them.

Press Ctrl and Alt together, then click inside your selection and drag a duplicate of the flower onto the green canvas. Release the mouse, then click and drag again several times to arrange the flowers on the canvas.

Reminder: Remember you can click **Ctrl-Z** to undo as many actions as you want!

Figure 2.9

● Save your picture as Daisies.

You can use the Magic Wand Tool to select the background colour. Then you can paint some shadows under the daisies using a soft brush, a slightly darker shade and a low opacity.

● Try creating some other masterpieces!

● Save and close the image when you're done.

Figure 2.10: Variations on a theme

Cloning

3

Cloning

The Clone Stamp Tool is a very powerful tool and one of the most used implements in the world of professional photo retouchers and computer artists.

You'll need to spend some time playing around with it to understand how it works.

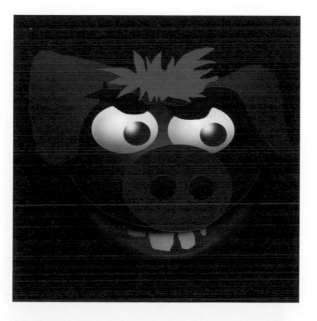

- ● Click on the background colour in the Toolbox and change it to a dark purple.

- ● Open a new canvas with dimensions 500 x 500 pixels, resolution 72 pixels/inch, mode RGB colour, contents background color.

We are going to make a cartoon mad pig's face, something like the one in Figure 3.1. We will start with the pig's eyes.

Figure 3.1

In the Toolbox, click the Marquee Tool and use the Ellipse option to draw an ellipse roughly where I have drawn the pig's left eye.

Choose a soft-edged Brush Tool and set the brush size to 100, opacity 100%. Spray the eye white.

Now we need a darker purple. Click the Set Foreground Color icon and the Color Picker window will appear. Move the cursor over the canvas and it will change to the Eyedropper icon. Click to set the foreground to the same colour as the background. Now you can drag the circular marker in the colour field to a darker hue. Close the Colour Picker window.

Reduce the size of the Brush Tool to 60 and carefully spray a shadow area at the bottom of the eye. I would set the opacity to 20 before you start to spray the shadow so you can build up the colour without overdoing it.

Tip: Opacity determines how 'thickly' the paint is laid on. The higher the opacity, the thicker the paint.

Deselect (Ctrl-D) and draw a circle selection to make the pupil. Colour it black, and think about where you are placing it because you could make a big difference in the character's expression!

Spray a white highlight over the pupil to give it a sparkle, make the brush size 30 and the opacity 100%. Just give it one burst of highlight.

Deselect by pressing Ctrl-D.

Figure 3.2

Using the Clone Stamp Tool

Using the Clone Stamp Tool you can paint an exact copy of any part of an image, either on a new canvas or on another part of the same canvas.

Now give it a go, following the instructions below.

▶ Click the Clone Stamp Tool in the Toolbox and set the Tool Options as shown in Figure 3.3.

Figure 3.3

▶ Press the Alt key and click somewhere in the pig's eye to activate the Clone Stamp Tool.

▶ Move the cursor to the position you want the coloured eye to go and start painting in small circles to clone the eye.

Figure 3.4: Starting to clone the eye

▶ Finish cloning the eye.

Don't worry if the eye is in the wrong position, we will now practice moving a selection.

Moving a selection

The eye in Figure 3.4 is too high, and needs to be moved.

 Use the Magic Wand Tool to select the white part of the right eye. Then hold down Shift while you select the pupil.

> **Tip:** Don't forget you can change the **Magic Wand** tolerance so you can more easily select the objects you want.

 Now click the Move Tool and move the eye. You should have something like Figure 3.5.

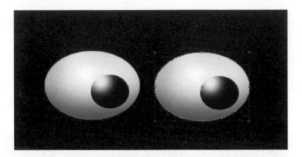

Figure 3.5: Moving a selection

> **Tip:** If you try and move the eye while the **Marquee Tool** is still selected, this will move only the selection area, not the eye. Don't forget to select the **Move Tool** first!

Around the eye you have moved it is quite usual to find the Magic Wand misses some of the selection so that a trace of the object is left in the original position. Also if your background colour has changed, there will be a different-coloured 'hole' left by the eye.

Figure 3.6

We can fix that now.

From the Select menu choose Inverse.

Using the Eyedropper Tool, click the purple canvas colour to set the foreground colour.

With the Brush Tool paint over the damage on the canvas, being careful not to paint the other eye.

Deselect by pressing Ctrl-D.

Subtracting selections

You already know how to add selections by holding down Shift as you make a second or third selection. You can also subtract portions of a selection by holding down the Alt key.

We will paint the mouth using this technique.

 ◉ Click the Elliptical Marquee Tool and draw a large circle selection from the left side of the left eye.

◉ Now hold the Alt key down and draw another ellipse starting from above the left eye.

The second circle has eaten away at the first, giving us a neat mouth shape.

◉ You can drag the selection, or use the arrow keys to move the selection if you need to. Using the Move Tool you can rotate the selection too.

Tip: To rotate an object with the **Move Tool**, you need to place the cursor just outside the corner of the selection box. The cursor will change to a bent double-headed arrow. Click and drag the selection to rotate.

Tip: You will have to have a good few goes to get a shape you like, but it's worth the effort.

Figure 3.7: Subtracting selections

◉ Spray the mouth dark purple and, decreasing the opacity to say 20, spray a small amount of the canvas colour on the bottom lip.

Tip: When you airbrush fine gradients build them up in fine layers and you will get a much better result.

Modifying a selection

Sometimes the selection area is almost, but not quite, what you want. You can modify it.

▶ From the Select menu choose Modify. Click Contract.

▶ Set the Contract Selection to 12 pixels. Click OK. You should see that the selection has got smaller.

▶ Go back to Select and this time select Feather. Set the Feather Radius to 3 pixels. This will give a soft edge to the selection.

▶ Colour the selection so that it looks something like Figure 3.8.

> **Note:** Notice the soft edge to the red mouth.

Figure 3.8: A contracted, feathered selection

 ▶ Now select the Lasso Tool and, holding down the Alt key, cut out some tombstone teeth like the ones in Figure 3.9.

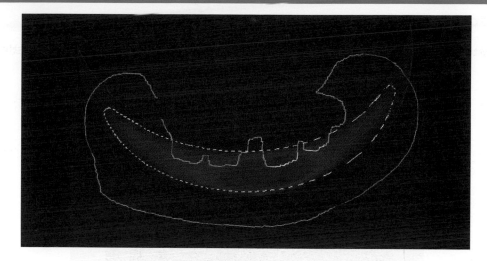

Figure 3.9

▶ Choosing the **Brush Tool** paint the teeth a grimy colour.

▶ Now using the **Elliptical Marquee Tool** draw the pig's nose, and then drag it slightly over the right eye.

▶ Colour it a lighter purple to match the background.

▶ Look at Figure 3.10. Draw and paint the right nostril using a circle or ellipse and carefully spray black around the top of it.

▶ We need another nostril so use the **Clone Stamp Tool** again.

If you look at Figure 3.10 you will see I have made the pig slightly 3-D on the face by spraying lighter purple above the nose and dark purple under it.

▶ Click the **Magic Wand Tool** and with the **tolerance** set very low, select the purple background.

▶ With the **Brush Tool** set to size **100** and opacity **15%**, spray light purple above the nose and dark under it.

Reminder: Don't forget the shortcut to deselect is **Ctrl-D**.

Finishing touches

You can use the Lasso Tool to add the ears, some manic eyebrows in black and lastly some hair.

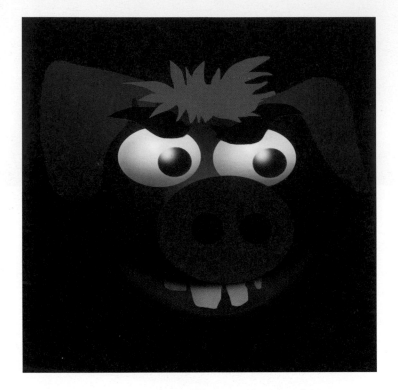

Figure 3.10

What a masterpiece!

▶ Save the image as Mad pig then close it.

Working with Layers

4

Layers are like transparent sheets arranged on top of each other. They can be arranged in different orders, and switched on and off. You can even make the layers react to different colours or contrasts and blend together to make some spectacular pictures.

Layers enable you to work on one element of your picture without changing the other elements and without having to make selections.

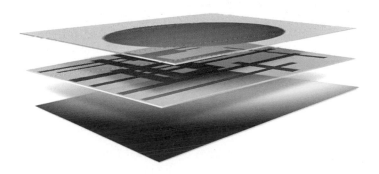

Figure 4.1

◉ Open a new canvas with dimensions 600 x 700 pixels, resolution 72 pixels/inch, mode RGB colour. Make the contents white and click OK.

Tip: You can't use layers with **Bitmap** or **Indexed Color** mode.

◉ Click on the Gradient Tool (under the T, fifth tool down on the right of the Toolbox) and have a look at the Options bar.

Figure 4.2

◉ Click Edit and choose one of the preset colour blends as shown in Figure 4.3.

Figure 4.3

To change the colour of a fill, click on a marker, then change the colour to either the foreground or background colour here.

Try clicking and dragging these markers to change the colour distribution of the fill.

▶ Click OK when you have some colours you are happy with.

▶ Make sure you have Linear Gradient selected on the Options bar.

▶ Click and drag the cursor across the canvas. You can experiment as many times as you like with different length lines and directions to achieve the effect you want.

Figure 4.4

Making a new layer

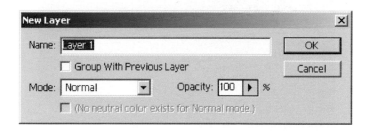

We need the Layers Palette so look in the Palette Well (top right) and click on Layers. Drag the Layers tab down into the work area so we can keep an eye on what is happening.

You may need to click and drag the box at the bottom right of the Layers Palette to expand the palette.

From the Menu bar select Layer, New, Layer.

In the New Layer dialogue box click OK.

Figure 4.5: The New Layer dialogue box

This is what you should see in the Layers Palette.

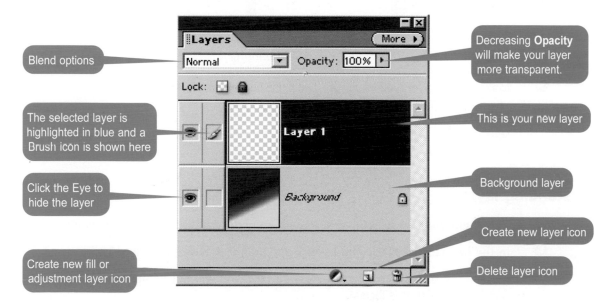

Figure 4.6: The Layers Palette

Make sure Layer 1 is selected in the Layers Palette. It should be highlighted blue – if it is not just click on it to select it.

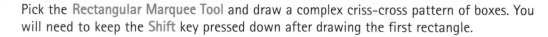

Pick the Rectangular Marquee Tool and draw a complex criss-cross pattern of boxes. You will need to keep the Shift key pressed down after drawing the first rectangle.

- With the Paint Bucket Tool pour a colour that really clashes with the background.
- Press Ctrl-D to deselect.

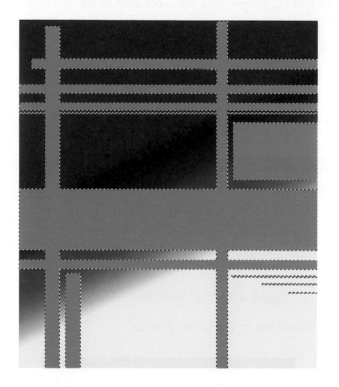

Figure 4.7: Filled pattern

- Make a new layer: you could use the Create a new layer icon.

- Make sure the new layer is selected in the Layers Palette (it will be coloured blue when selected) and draw a large circle right in the middle of the canvas using the marque tool. Colour it black.

Understanding layers

We'll experiment with these two layers to gain an understanding of how they work.

- In the Layers Palette, click on Layer 2 and drag it down below Layer 1.

The black circle is now under the criss-cross pattern. You will not be able to put it under the background layer, as that is locked.

- Click the Eye icon and switch off and on all the layers. You will notice Photoshop shows a checker-board pattern as the background to each layer to show there is nothing there.

- With Layer 2 selected, pick the Move Tool and move the circle anywhere you like. Try moving Layer 1 as well – you will see that each layer can be moved or shuffled in any order you like.

▷ Now use the Opacity slider in the Layers Palette and experiment with the layers. Set them both to 100 when you are finished.

Figure 4.8: Layer opacity

▷ Lastly, experiment with the Blending Mode, currently set to Normal. Click Layer 1 and change the Blending Mode to Difference.

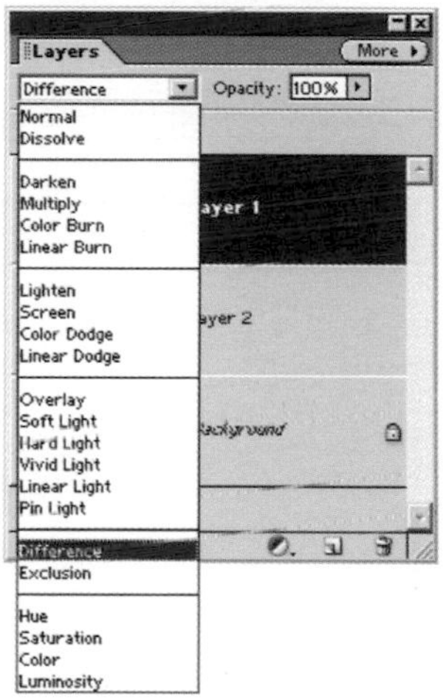

Figure 4.9: Blending modes

▷ Experiment by changing the blending mode in both the layers.

Figure 4.10

Try making some other funky backgrounds!

▷ Save the image as Background then close it.

Editing a library image using layers

Supplied with the Photoshop Elements program CD are some pictures already in digital form. In the next project we will use one of them.

○ If you have the Photoshop Elements CD, insert it into the CD drive.

You will see the CD will try to install the software again. Simply hit the Close button in the top right of the Title screen.

○ Select File, Browse from the Menu bar or use the icon on the Shortcuts bar.

○ Click My Computer in the top left box and the Elements CD will be visible on the right.

○ Double-click on the Elements CD and you will see Goodies at the bottom.

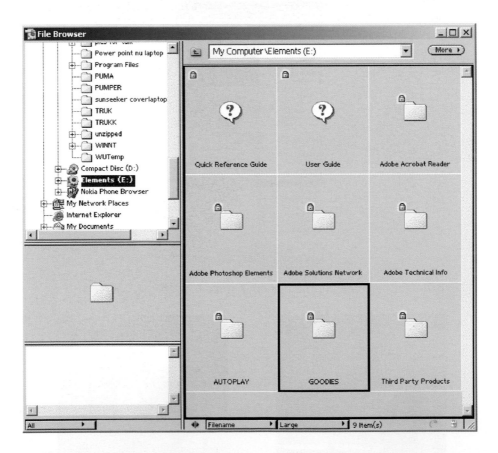

Figure 4.11: Browsing to find an image

Tip: If you are working on a network, you may not have the CD to insert. The image you need may be downloaded from **www.payne-gallway.co.uk/elements** and stored in a suitable folder.

○ Double-click Goodies, then Stock art, then Images and look for image 0006753. jpg.

◉ Open 0006753.jpg by double-clicking its icon.

◉ Click the Maximize icon and have a look at the picture.

Figure 4.12: Image 0006753.jpg

We are going to change this snowy scene into a Spring day. We need to think about perspective and shadow direction for maximum artistic effect.

Transforming the picture

First we need to duplicate it so we always have a copy of the untouched picture.

◉ From the Menu bar select Layer, Duplicate Layer.

◉ Leave the name as Background copy and click OK.

A useful way of enhancing dull or faded pictures is to use Auto Contrast or Auto Levels.

◉ Make sure the Background copy layer is selected in the Layers Palette and then from the Menu bar choose Enhance, Auto Levels.

> **Tip:** The **Enhance** options all work slightly differently, so sometimes it is useful to run each one and then undo to see which works the best.

Use the Clone Stamp Tool to paint out the shadow to the left of the foreground tree. (Use a small brush with Opacity set to 100%.)

Figure 4.13

At the bottom of the Layers Palette is the Create new fill or adjustment layer icon. Click it and choose Hue/Saturation. Copy the settings in Figure 4.14 – make sure you check the Colorize box.

Figure 4.14: Hue and Saturation

Click OK.

From the Layers menu select New, Layer and call the layer grass.

Tip: Alternatively, you could click the **Create a new layer** icon in the **Layers Palette**. Double-click the **layer thumbnail** (where it says **Layer 1**) to get an information box where you can name the layer.

Choose the Brush Tool and the Grass brush (near the bottom of the Default Brushes list).

The Grass brush uses a mix between the foreground and background colours, so select a bright green for the foreground and a darker green for the background and that will give us some variation in grass colour.

On the grass layer, paint grass all over the field. Look at Figure 4.15 for inspiration – I have used grass at 15 pixels, 40% opacity in the distance and 100 pixels, 50% opacity in the foreground.

Figure 4.15

Add some coloured dots in clumps: they will look like flowers and really help finish the picture.

Create a new layer and call it sky.

Select the Lasso Tool, and change the lasso option Feather to 5 pixels (this will soften the selection), and draw a selection around the hedgerow and around the sky.

With the Brush Tool paint in a sky like Figure 4.16. Press Ctrl-D to deselect.

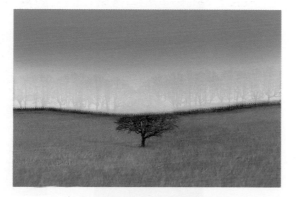

Figure 4.16

In the Layers Palette change the Blend Mode from Normal to Color.

○ ▸ Add a new layer and call it sun. Paint the sun in the top right with a large soft brush, like Figure 4.17.

Figure 4.17

○ ▸ Nearly there! We need to add leaves to the trees, so create a new layer called background trees.

○ ▸ Select the Brush Tool and choose the Scattered Maple Leaves brush.

Before painting the trees we need to think about light and shadow. Look at Figure 4.18 and notice how I have put a highlight on the leaves around the edge facing the sun and darkened the area away from the light source. Try to use this technique when you paint the row of trees in the background. We will paint the tree in front of the field in a little while.

○ ▸ Choose foreground and background leaf colours to suit the areas you are going to paint. Do all the dark areas first and work around to the highlights, setting the brush to 8 pixels and 70% opacity.

Tip: Don't forget to zoom in so you can more accurately paint the leaves.
When you are zoomed in, use the **Hand Tool** to scroll across the canvas; you can press the **Spacebar** as a shortcut.

Figure 4.18: Adding shadows and highlights

> Make a new layer called foreground trees and paint the foreground tree, setting the brush size to 20 pixels and leaving the opacity at 70%.

Adding Shadows

The last layer is the shadows layer. The trees will cast shadows across the field – have a look at figure 4.20 for reference.

> Create a new layer called shadows.

> Select a very dark green Scattered maple leaves brush, and use the same settings as before i.e. 8 pixels and 70% opacity for the background trees.

> In the Layers Palette change the Blend Mode from Normal to Multiply and use the Opacity slider to create the perfect shadow density. Paint the shadows onto the field.

> Drag the Shadows layer under the Background trees layer.

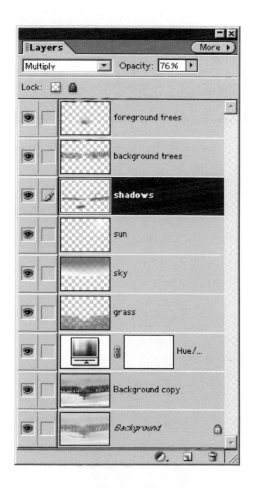

Figure 4.19

Figure 4.20: The finished job

▶   Save your masterpiece as Trees.

Tip: If you get a message about permission to save, it is probably because you are trying to save to the CD. Check the save location then try again.

▶   Try switching the different layers on and off so you can see the difference you have made.

You could add some birds or try painting some clouds in. You can use the Hue and Saturation to tweak the colours on each layer – to do this, go to Enhance, Adjust Color, Hue/Saturation.

▶   When you've finished save the image then close it.

▶   Close the Browse Files window if it is still open by clicking the Close icon at the top right of the screen in the Menu bar.

Vector Graphics

Raster or bitmap images are made up from an array of different-coloured pixels. The resolution of a picture is measured typically in pixels per inch (ppi) or dots per inch (dpi), and the more pixels per inch, the finer the detail in the picture. Raster images are very good for storing and changing photographic style pictures but if you enlarge the image, the results will probably not be satisfactory and individual pixels will be visible.

Vector images are made from mathematical information about the curves, sizes, point positions and colours. Whenever you change the size of a vector image, rotate or skew it, the image is redrawn and will be perfect. This type of image is good for graphical shapes or text. We are now going to create a vector image.

Rabbit

○ Choose a light grey in the Set background color box.

○ Open a new canvas 600 pixels wide and 800 high, mode RGB Color. Check the Background Color box.

○ Right-click the fourth spot down on the left of the Toolbox. From the list that appears select the Shape Selection Tool. Next time you need this tool you can just left-click with the mouse on this icon in the Toolbox.

	Rectangle Tool	U
	Rounded Rectangle Tool	U
	Ellipse Tool	U
	Polygon Tool	U
	Line Tool	U
	Custom Shape Tool	U
■	Shape Selection Tool	U

Choose the Ellipse Tool from the Options bar and draw an ellipse in the center of the canvas.

After you have drawn the ellipse you can change its colour by clicking in the Color box on the Options bar.

Click the Colour box and choose a mid grey.

It is easy to alter a shape that you have drawn by applying transformations to it.

Near the left-hand end of the Options bar is the Shape Selection Tool. Click the ellipse you have drawn and you will get a Transform box, and then you can move the nodes or the whole object.

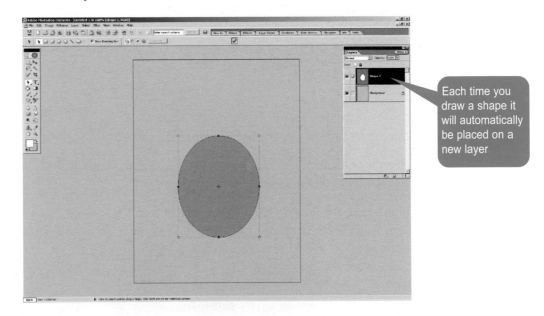

> Each time you draw a shape it will automatically be placed on a new layer

Figure 5.1

When you have finished moving and resizing the ellipse, click the Commit Transform icon in the Options bar.

When the Commit Transform icon has been clicked, it is replaced with the Dismiss Target Path icon (they look very similar!).

Tip: When you use **Ctrl/Alt** to duplicate you can also press the **Shift** key and this will lock the duplicated shape in a horizontal or vertical plane.

○ You will need to click the Dismiss Target Path icon when you have finished moving and resizing the ellipse.

The ellipse you have just drawn is going to be the rabbit's head. We are going to add his eyes next.

○ Draw in a nice big white eye as in Figure 5.2.

○ Position it with the Shape Selection Tool.

○ Use the Ctrl/Alt keys to duplicate the eye onto the same layer.

Don't forget: after duplicating and moving the ellipse you must click the Commit Transform icon then the Dismiss Target Path icon in the Options bar. If you can't see these icons, click the Shape Selection Tool in the Options bar.

○ Draw another ellipse to make the pupil and colour it black. Copy it into the other eye.

Figure 5.2

○ Follow the instructions as labelled in Figure 5.3.

Draw this second, duplicate it and that will be part of his nose.

This will be the last circle. It's the rabbit's nose.

Draw this ellipse first, duplicate it and that will be his cheeks.

Figure 5.3

Tip: When you draw the rabbit's nose, draw the ellipse and before you release the mouse button, press the **Shift** key to constrain its proportions. It will be a perfect circle.

▷ Draw another ellipse and colour it purple to make the rabbit's mouth. You will notice it is over the top of the nose, so in the Layers Palette drag the layer down under the pink part of the nose as in Figure 5.4. Unless you have named each layer after drawing every ellipse your layers will be called quite unhelpful names like Shape 1, Shape 2 etc. You may need to experiment a little with the position of the mouth layer in the Layers Palette to locate it in front of the cheeks but behind the nose.

Tip: To make re-ordering the layers easier, try naming the **nose**, **mouth** and **cheeks** layers. To do this, click on a shape using the **Shape Selection Tool** and open the **Layers Palette**. The selected layer will be highlighted blue. Double-click the existing layer name and enter a new name. Now you can see exactly where the mouth needs to be positioned – because you know which layer corresponds to which shape.

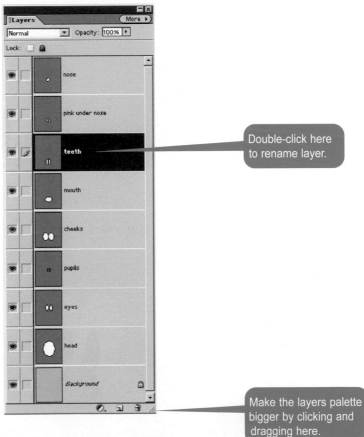

Double-click here to rename layer.

Make the layers palette bigger by clicking and dragging here.

Figure 5.4: The Layers Palette

Next, use the rounded rectangle tool to make some light yellow teeth. Slightly rotate the teeth to make them look more buck.

Figure 5.5: The rabbit so far

Tip: To move or rotate an object using the **Shape Selection Tool**, you need to click it twice so that the **Transform box** appears around the object.

Copying and pasting objects

Now you need to draw the ears.

○ Draw and position the first ear shape.

○ To get the same colour as you used for the face, double-click the Layer Thumbnail icon for the ear, and the Color Picker window will appear. Move the cursor over the rabbit and the cursor will change into an Eyedropper icon. Click on the mid-gray of the rabbit's head, and click OK in the Color Picker window.

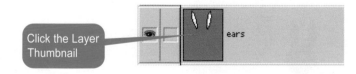

Figure 5.6

○ Click the Shape Selection Tool. Click the ear shape once so that it gets a darker outline. Click again and the Transform box will appear around the ear. Now select Edit, Copy from the menu.

○ Select Edit, Paste. The pasted copy will appear on top of the donor ellipse so you won't be able to see it.

Click and drag it and rotate it into position. Click the Commit Transform icon.

Figure 5.7: Ear we go

   Click the Dismiss Target Path icon; you will notice that both ear shapes are in the same layer.

Make two more pinky ellipses to put inside the ears.

Make a droopy ear with another ellipse the same colour as the ears, and make sure it goes over the top of the pink inside ear.

See if you can add some whiskers!

> Double-click the **Layer Thumbnail** icon to change the colours or just tweak them slightly.

> Here all the layers have been named – don't worry if your Layers Palette looks different. Unless you've renamed your layers they will be called something like **Shape 1**, **Shape 2** etc.

Figure 5.8

You will probably find that some of your objects are not quite correctly positioned.

○ Use the Shape Selection Tool to select an object that you want to move, and click it a second time to transform or move the shape.

Tip: Remember that you can select several shapes at once (if they are on the same layer) by holding down **Shift** while you select each one.

○ Save the image as Surprised bunny1.psd. We will need this version of the bunny later so don't save over it. We'll create a second copy of it to work on now by saving it as a different name.

○ Select File, Save As from the menu and this time give it the file name Surprised bunny2.psd.

Tip: You don't need to enter **.psd** in the **File name** box. Just make sure the **Format** selected is **Photoshop**, and the **.psd** file extension will be added automatically when you save it.

Layer Styles

Right, now let's add some fantastic layer styles – these can transform your vector illustration in moments.

○ Start by selecting the teeth. Just click on a tooth with the Shape Selection Tool.

○ Find Layer Styles located in the Palette Well.

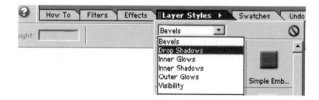

○ Click it and choose Drop Shadows from the pull-down menu. Choose Low.

○ Isn't that great? Apply the same drop shadow to the pink under the nose.

○ Click the mouth, and from the Layer Styles palette, select Inner Shadows, High.

○ Next click on the round red nose, and from the Layer Styles palette choose Wow Plastic. Pick a colored plastic nose.

Look in the nose Layer and you will notice a little f symbol on the right-hand side.

Double-click this symbol to edit the **Layer Style** settings.

○ Double-click the f symbol or select Layer, Layer Style, Style Settings from the Menu bar.

○ Copy the settings in Figure 5.9.

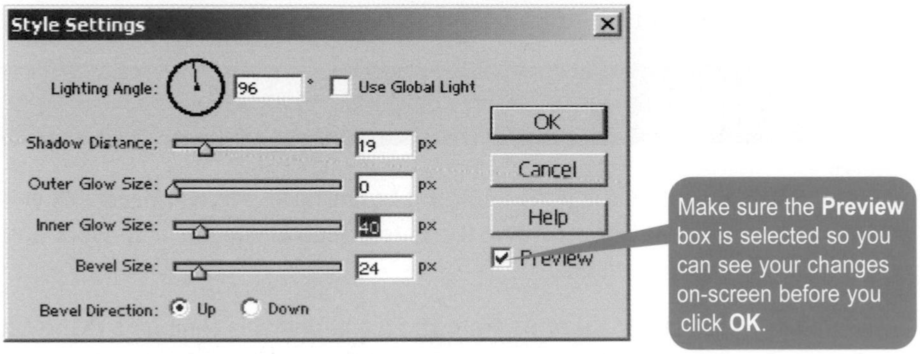

Figure 5.9: Style settings

Have a play with the settings to see what they do. Lighting angle controls the light source direction, and the shadow distance will increase or decrease the amount of shadow you will see. The bevel size will help give your object a real 3D quality so always adjust it to achieve the best possible effect.

○ Click the white of the eyes and apply Wow Plastic Grey. Apply the settings in Figure 5.10.

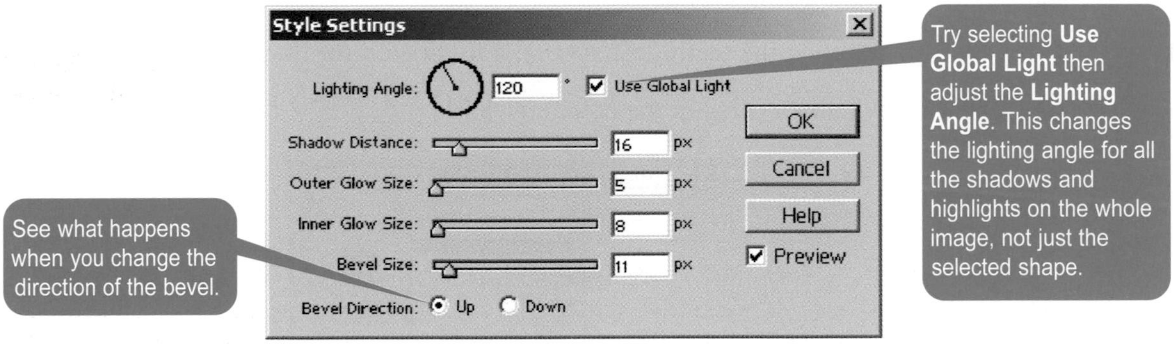

Figure 5.10: Settings for the eyes

○ Click OK.

○ Save the image as Surprised bunny2.psd, but don't close it just yet.

Figure 5.11: The finished bunny

Vector vs. Raster images

When you draw a shape like an ellipse or write some text using the Type Tool, the shapes and text are Vector graphics. When you use the paintbrush to spray a bit of paint on the canvas, this is a Raster image.

Enlarging or resizing

Vector images are independent of resolution; the computer remembers the geometrical information associated with that shape, and if the resolution or image size is changed, the shape can simply be redrawn with no loss of image quality. The extra information that allows the software to do this is called embedded information.

Raster images, because they are stored as a collection of different-coloured pixels will become pixelated if they are enlarged too much. This is why you should always enlarge a vector image to its final size before you turn it into a raster image, not after.

The bunny image is a Vector image. The Starry night image you created in Chapter 1 is a Raster image. We'll look at what happens when we zoom in and resize each image.

▶   Open both these images now. Your Surprised bunny2.psd image might already be open.

▶   Zoom in on both pictures in turn, as far as the zoom will go.

You will see that both images have pixelated edges. This is because computer monitors display images on a grid made up of pixels, which means that although vector images should appear with perfect smooth edges, the data is displayed as pixels on the screen.

Now see what happens when we make the canvas size bigger:

▶   Start with Starry night. Select Image, Resize, Image Size from the Menu bar.

▶   Copy the settings at the top of Figure 5.12 (width and height). Click OK.

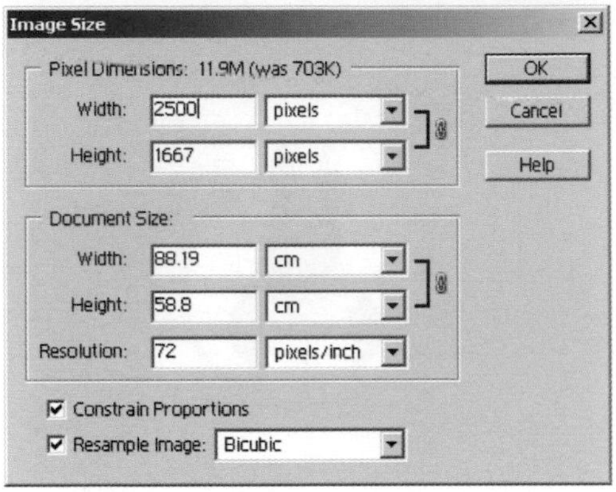

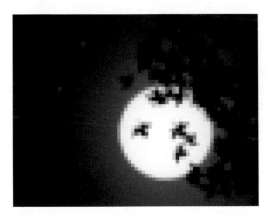

Figure 5.12: Image size settings for a raster image

Figure 5.13: The raster image is blurred

The image has jumped up in size. Notice that the image is quite blurred. This is because to show the raster image at this size, Photoshop divided up the existing pixels, since there is no more information stored in the image.

▶   Now click on the Surprised bunny2 image. Select Image, Resize, Image Size from the Menu bar.

○ Copy the settings in Figure 5.14.

Figure 5.14: Image size settings for vector image

○ Zoom in and have a look.

Figure 5.15: The vector image is sharp even after resizing

The edges are still sharp, as the shape information embedded in the vector image has been used to redraw the image at the larger size.

○ Close both images without saving.

Converting vector graphics into raster images

There are certain things that you can't do with vector graphics though, which is why we sometimes need to simplify a layer or flatten an image. This simply means you are turning it into a raster layer, or raster image. When you do this, the software remembers which colour was in which pixel; it no longer knows where one shape ends and another one starts.

If you imagine a vector image being a pile of shapes that can be individually picked up and moved around, turning that vector image into a raster image is like taking a photo of all the shapes: the image looks the same, but now you can't pick up and move individual shapes.

Effects

6

By adding different effects to a picture you can create some spectacular results very quickly. You can also transform a photograph into something quite different! In this chapter you will be mixing vector and raster images and applying effects to them.

Experimenting with effects

▶ Create a new canvas 850 pixels wide and high, specifying Mode as RGB Color and Contents as White.

We are going to make a background that looks like brushed steel.

▶ Select Filter, Noise, Add Noise from the Menu bar. Copy the settings in Figure 6.1. (You can experiment with different settings, and the Preview box will allow you to see what is happening).

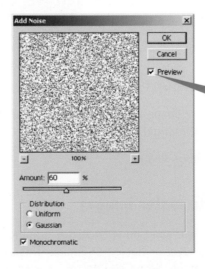

Click the **Preview** box and this will allow you to see what is happening in real time. You may need to click and drag the blue title bar at the top of the **Add Noise** dialogue box to move it if it is in front of the image.

Figure 6.1: The Add Noise dialogue box

▶ Click OK.

▷ Now select Filter, Blur, Motion Blur from the Menu bar. Copy the settings in Figure 6.2. Click OK.

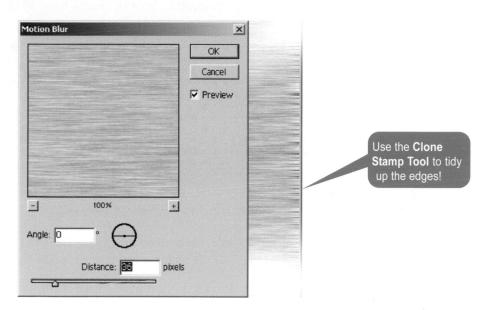

Use the **Clone Stamp Tool** to tidy up the edges!

Figure 6.2: The Motion Blur dialogue box

Custom Shape Tool

Before we start, we need to make a new layer. We will then design an industrial-looking logo.

▷ Make sure the Layers Palette is open; if it isn't, click and drag it from the Palette Well onto the workspace. Create a new layer by clicking the New Layer icon at the bottom of the Layers Palette.

▷ Click the Shape Tool (fourth spot down on the left of the Toolbox) then select the Custom Shape Tool in the Options bar.

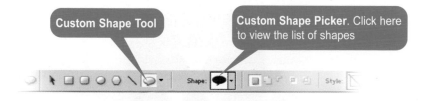

Custom Shape Tool

Custom Shape Picker. Click here to view the list of shapes

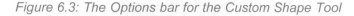

Figure 6.3: The Options bar for the Custom Shape Tool

Tip: Instead of clicking the **Shape Tool** and choosing the **Custom Shape Tool** try just pressing **U** on the keyboard.

▶ Click the small down-arrow on the Custom Shape Picker (see Figure 6.3) and a window will roll down. Click the small arrow in the top right-hand corner and choose the All Elements Shapes option. You will be able to choose from all these vector shapes:

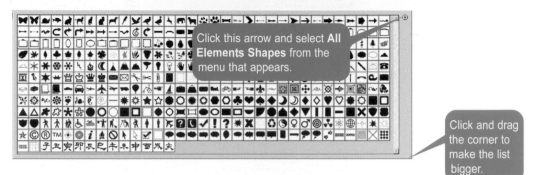

Figure 6.4: The Custom Shape Picker

▶ Using Figure 6.5 as a guide, try to draw a logo like the one shown, putting each shape on a separate layer. Leave out the shadow for now, we'll add that in a minute.

ℹ Double-click the Layer Thumbnail (the small image to the left of the layer name in the Layers Palette) to open the colour picker for that shape.

ℹ Don't forget you can change the layer order by clicking and dragging the layers up and down in the Layers Palette.

> **Tip:** When you draw a shape, you can press the **Shift** key to constrain its proportions. If you also press the **Alt** key the shape will draw from the position where you click and will expand from that central point. You can use both keys at the same time.

▶ Use the Move Tool to tweak the size and position of the shape in the current layer.

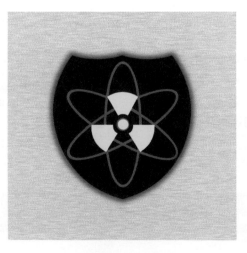

Figure 6.5: The logo

○ Select the shield background shape by clicking it in the Layers Palette. Click the Layer Styles Palette in the Palette Well. Select Drop Shadows from the drop-down menu, then click the first option, High.

 ○ Double-click the f icon in the Layers Palette to edit the layer style we've just applied. Set the Style Settings as shown in Figure 6.6 so the drop shadow makes a feathered dark edge all the way round the shape.

Style Settings

Lighting Angle: 120 °   ☑ Use Global Light

Shadow Distance: ⌐————————— |1   px

Outer Glow Size: ⌐———————— |0   px

Inner Glow Size: ⌐———————— |0   px

Bevel Size: ⌐————————— |0   px

Bevel Direction: ○ Up   ○ Down

OK
Cancel
Help
☑ Preview

Figure 6.6: Settings for the drop shadow

We need to merge all the layers into one for the next section, but before doing this we'll save a layered version.

○ Save your image as Logo with layers, making sure the file format is Photoshop.

○ Save the image a second time, this time with the name Logo flattened.

Flattening images

The next step is to turn the artwork into a raster file as it is currently a vector file. In a raster file there are no layers and no individual shapes. Turning a vector file into a raster file involves merging all the layers and shapes. The image will look the same, but the things you can do to it will change.

○ Select Layer, Flatten Image from the Menu bar. You will also find a Flatten Image option on the top right pull-out menu in the Layers Palette.

Now comes the fun part! We are going to use the Photoshop Renderer to get great results by applying an embossed effect.

Texture maps & Bump maps

To create an embossed look Photoshop needs to raise certain parts of the image. You can choose how Photoshop selects which parts of the image to raise; here we want different parts of the image to be raised according to how much red there is in the image.

To do this Photoshop needs to create a Texture Map based on the contents of the Red channel. Each image is made up of three colours, Red, Green and Blue. Each of these colours has its own channel and Photoshop can easily split these channels and look at the distribution of just one colour in an image.

Texture Maps (sometimes called Bump Maps) are used in the world of 3D modelling to add detail to 3D models. The Texture Map works by converting the colour channel into a greyscale image and then using that image to emboss the dark areas more than the light areas. Don't worry if you don't understand this – just follow the steps below!

Adding a lighting effect

It's always a good idea to make a backup of the layer you are altering in case anything goes wrong and you want to start again.

▷ Look at the blue title bar of the image that you are working on; make sure it's the Logo flattened file not the Logo with layers file.

▷ Right-click the background layer in the Layers Palette and choose Duplicate Layer to make the backup. Leave the name as Background copy.

▷ Select Filter, Render, Lighting Effects from the Menu bar.

▷ Copy the settings in Figure 6.7.

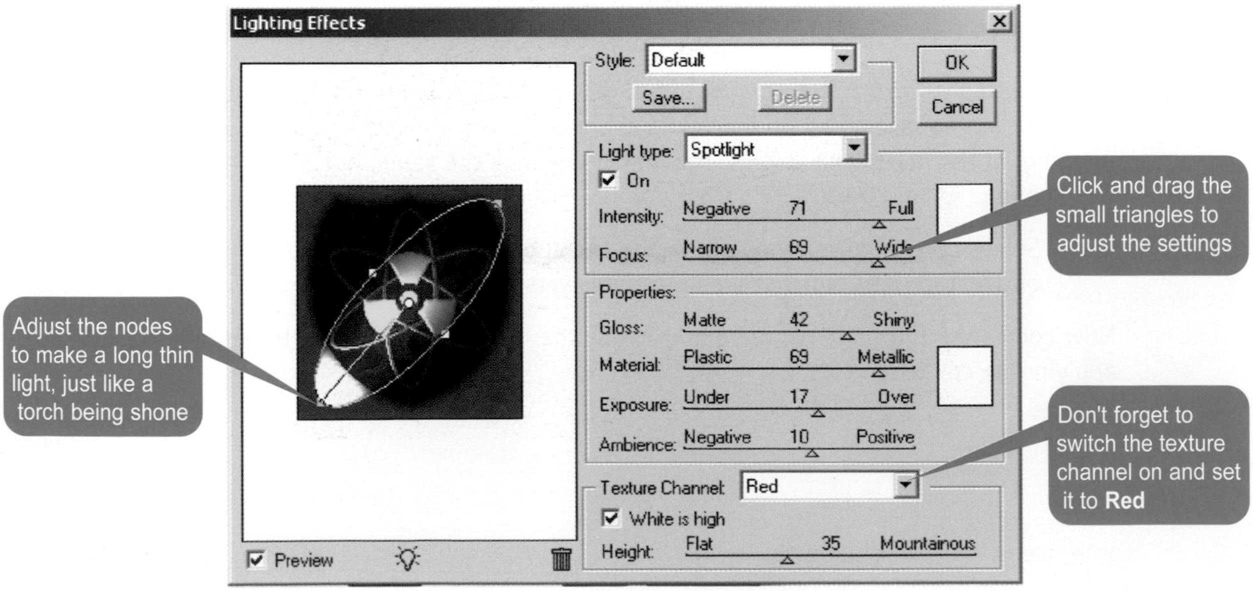

Figure 6.7: Lighting Effects

○ Click OK.

Figure 6.8: The final image

This effect has given the logo a very realistic 3D look!

○ Select File, Save from the Menu bar, then close the image.

Applying effects to photographs

○ Open image 0004678.jpg from the Photoshop CD. All the images we use in this book that are on the Elements CD are in the folder Goodies, Stock Art, Images. If you don't have the CD you can download the image from www.payne-gallway.co.uk/elements.

Figure 6.9: Image 0004678.jpg on the Elements CD

Now we have the skyline picture open, we will apply some effects to dramatically change it.

○ Duplicate the layer so that you have an untouched version you can revert to and compare with your new version.

Adjusting the brightness and contrast

We will start by altering the contrast of the picture, making it darker but still keeping the building lights bright.

▶   Select Enhance, Adjust Brightness/Contrast, Brightness/Contrast from the Menu bar.

▶   Copy the settings in Figure 6.10 then click OK.

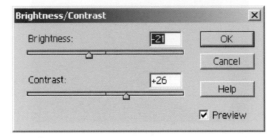

Figure 6.10: Brightness/Contrast window

▶   Now let's add a rising sun. Select Filter, Render, Lens Flare from the Menu bar.

Figure 6.11: The Lens Flare window

▶   Left-click and drag the crosshair to position the Lens Flare between the buildings.

▶   Set the flare to 105mm Prime. Try the other flares to see the difference, pressing Ctrl-Z or the Step Backward icon to undo anything you don't like.

Well, that gives a real zing to the picture!

Now let's give it quite a different effect to make it look rather like an electronic circuit board.

▶   Select Filter, Brush Strokes, Ink Outlines from the Menu bar. Experiment with different settings, viewing them in the Preview window.

▶   When you have tried out some different settings, enter the settings shown in Figure 6.12 and click OK.

▶   Save your image as Patchwork skyline, but don't close it yet.

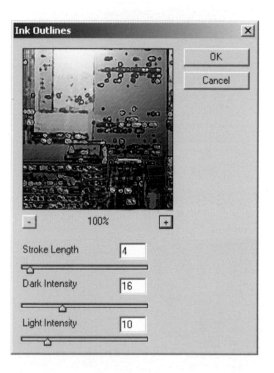

Figure 6.12: Ink outlines

Pretty wacky and very cool... let's use one more filter.

▶   Select Filter, Texture, Patchwork from the Menu bar.

◐ Copy Figure 6.13 then click OK.

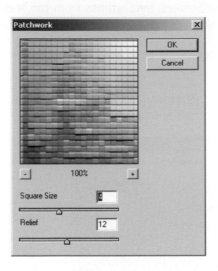

Figure 6.13: Patchwork filter

Now you know where designers have been getting their great images for magazines and other publications!

Figure 6.14: The finished scene!

◐ Select File, Print Preview from the Menu bar.

◐ From the Print Preview window click the Page Setup button to change the paper orientation if needed. Close the Page Setup window by clicking OK.

◐ Either click the Print button to print, or just close the Print Preview window without printing by clicking OK.

◐ You should have already saved your image as Patchwork skyline. To save again under the same file name just click the Save icon on the Shortcuts bar. Close the image – all done.

Text and Effects

In Photoshop Elements you use the horizontal and vertical Type Tools to create and edit text. Each of the Type Tools has a variety of settings in the Options bar, allowing you to select the font, style, size and colour.

Clicking in an image with a Type Tool puts the Type Tool in edit mode so that you can enter new text and edit existing text.

Once you create a Type layer, you can edit the text and apply layer commands to it (such as Layer Styles). You can change the orientation of the type and warp it into a variety of shapes – so there is plenty of scope for interesting effects!

Let's look at some funky text projects.

Creating the background

- ⊙ Open a new canvas 400 pixels wide by 80 high, RGB Colour and White background.

- ⊙ Choose a mid-blue foreground colour and paint the canvas using the Paint Bucket Tool.

- ⊙ Duplicate the background layer by right-clicking the layer in the Layers Palette and selecting Duplicate Layer from the shortcut menu that appears. Name the new layer Button.

> **Tip:** You need to duplicate the layer because the filter we will use makes part of the image transparent.

- ⊙ Open the Layer Styles Palette from the Palette Well if it is not already open and choose Wow Plastic from the drop-down list. Select the Aqua Blue colour.

Double-click the f icon in the Layers Palette and customize the effect using the settings shown in Figure 7.1.

Figure 7.1: Style Settings dialogue box

Adding text

Click the Type Tool in the Toolbox and copy the settings in the Options bar shown in Figure 7.2.

Try clicking Anti-aliased on and off. You will notice this smoothes the edges of the type, so keep it on.

Set the Text Colour to blue so it will match the background.

Figure 7.2 Type options

Now click in the middle of your canvas. You will notice that a Type layer has been automatically added to the Layers Palette.

Type my web site.

Using the Move Tool, move the text to the center of the canvas. Use the nodes to stretch the text across the button.

Click the Commit Transform icon.

▶ With the Type layer highlighted in the Layers Palette, select Wow Plastic from the Layer Styles Palette. Choose the Dark Blue colour. Copy the style settings in Figure 7.3, then click OK.

> **Tip:** Remember that to open the **Style Settings** dialogue box you need to double-click the **f icon** in the **Layers Palette**.

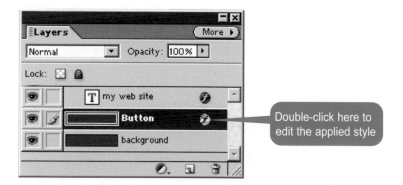

Figure 7.3: Effects applied to text

▶ Click the Button layer, then open the Layer Styles Palette. Try out some different styles!

The finished button:

Figure 7.4: Applying a different style to the button

Experiment with some more effects if you like. When you're done, save the image as button, then close it.

Adding perspective to text

This is a short exercise that uses the Free Transform options. We will add a piece of text to a mailbox, keeping it in perspective.

▷   Open image 0006519.jpg from the Photoshop CD, or download it from www.payne-gallway.co.uk/elements.

Figure 7.5: Image 0006519.jpg

▷   Select the Type Tool from the Toolbox and copy the settings for the Options bar below.

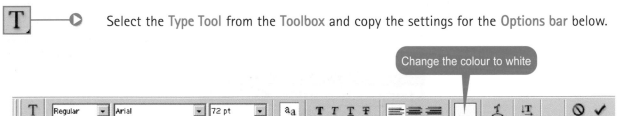

Figure 7.6: Text Options

Tip: The options that appear in the first drop-down list (where it says **Regular** in the screenshot) change according to which font is selected. Because of this, you need to select **Arial** before specifying **Regular**.

▷   Click on the canvas and type A Smith.

▷   With your new Type layer selected (click it in the Layers Palette to make sure) go to Image, Transform, Free Transform.

▷   Click and drag the nodes around the text to make your text nice and big, holding down the Shift key to keep the text proportions.

▷   Click the Commit Transform icon or press the Enter key.

Simplifying a Type layer

Select Image, Transform from the Menu bar and you will notice there are two options greyed out; unfortunately we want one of them! These options won't work unless the layer is simplified, but once the layer is simplified we won't be able to edit the text using the Type Tool. We can still pull it around and add effects though.

▶   Select Layer, Simplify Layer from the Menu bar.

Distorting text

▶   Select Image, Transform, Distort from the Menu bar. Click and drag the nodes to look like Figure 7.7.

Tip: Make sure the sides of the transformation box run with the perspective of the mail box. Zoom in to position the nodes more accurately. The better you line up the box with the photo, the more realistic it will look.

Figure 7.7: Distorting text

▶   Click the Commit Transform icon.

▶   In the Layers Palette, bring the Opacity down to 85%: that should really make the new text look part of the image.

Figure 7.8: Finished mail box with text

▶   Save the image as Mail box.psd, then close it.

Mixing text and filters

One of the easiest ways to make text interesting is to have different text sizes and to add filters to parts of it. This adds movement to the text.

▶ Open a new canvas, 800 pixels wide by 300 high, RGB Color and White background.

▶ Click the Type Tool in the Toolbox. Copy the settings in Figure 7.9 to the Options bar. Click anywhere in the canvas and write The Time Machine.

You might not have this font. If you don't it doesn't matter, just choose another one that you like.

Figure 7.9: Type options

▶ Use the Move Tool to reposition the text in the middle of the canvas. Adjust the size of the text if you need to so that it easily fits on the canvas.

▶ With the Type Tool click on the right side of the e of Time and drag the selection back to select the entire word (alternatively, double-click the word Time). In the Options bar, increase the size of the font so that the word Time is much bigger than the other words (see Figure 7.10).

▶ If you need to, use the Move Tool again to center the text on the canvas.

Now we'll add the background effect.

▶ Click the Background layer in the Layers Palette. Now select Effects from the Palette Well; double-click Psychedelic Strings.

Look in the Layers Palette. This effect has been inserted as another layer above the background layer. It's a good idea to name the layer something meaningful.

Figure 7.10

Simplifying a layer

○ Right-click the text layer in the Layers Palette and select Simplify Layer from the menu that appears.

> **Tip:** Once we simplify the text layer, all the embedded information will be lost. This means that if we dramatically enlarge the text it will degrade the image. Always try and resize the text to the correct size before you simplify a layer.

We can now select individual words or letters as objects to pull around.

 ○ Check that the text layer is selected in the Layers Palette. Use the Rectangle Marquee Tool to select the word Time by drawing a rectangle around it.

We will now make the word Time look as if it is at an angle.

○ Select Image, Transform, Perspective from the Menu bar. Move the nodes on the right-hand side of the perspective box closer together.

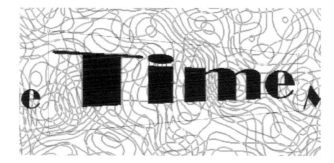

> **Tip: Perspective** will give the impression the word is vanishing into the distance.

○ Now select Image, Transform, Distort from the Menu bar. Try to copy the image below.

> **Tip: Distort** will give you a lot more options but is more difficult to get right than **Perspective**.

○ Click the Commit Transform icon.

○ Keep the word selected because we will now add some effects to it. Select Filter, Stylize, Emboss from the Menu bar. Copy the options in Figure 7.11, then click OK.

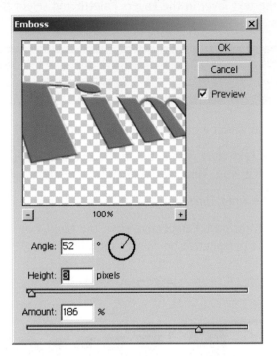

Figure 7.11

Applying the Motion Blur filter

○ Deselect the text (Ctrl-D) then select the Lasso Tool; draw a wide selection around the word Time.

○ Select Filter, Blur, Motion Blur from the Menu bar. Set the Angle to 4 degrees and the Distance to 10 pixels.

Figure 7.12: Finished!

○ Deselect by pressing Ctrl-D.

○ Save the image as The Time Machine then close it.

Combining Text and Graphics

8

In this chapter we will combine text and graphics to create a party flyer, a picture montage and a book cover.

Making a club night flyer

 ○ Open image 0006758.jpg from the Photoshop CD, or download it from www.payne-gallway.co.uk/elements.

Figure 8.1: Image 0006758.jpg

We can make the breaking wave a bit more interesting and funky by applying a filter.

○ Duplicate the layer by right-clicking on it in the Layers Palette, then selecting Duplicate Layer from the shortcut menu.

○   Select Filter, Distort, Ocean Ripple from the Menu bar. Set the Ripple Size and the Ripple Magnitude to 9 and click OK.

○   In the Blend Mode drop-down list (in the top left of the Layers Palette) select Lighten.

> **Tip:** Just after you have changed the layer blend options you will notice that the option will be highlighted in blue. When this is highlighted you can scroll through the other options simply by using the **Up/Down** cursor keys.

Adding text

○   Next, select the Vertical Type Tool from the Type Tool options in the Options bar. Alternatively you can click and hold the Type Tool in the Toolbox and select it from there.

○   Match the options to the ones shown in Figure 8.2.

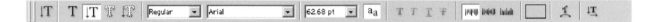

Figure 8.2: Vertical Type Options

○   Click the top left-hand corner of the canvas and type Beach Party.

○   Use the Move Tool to make the text a bit wider. Click the Commit Transform icon.

Figure 8.3

▶ From the Layer Styles Palette select Wow Chrome, Wow Chrome Shiny Edge.

▶ Now is a good time to make sure you have named your layers as we will be using several layers in this project. Notice that the text layer already has some of the text added so you won't need to rename that one. Rename the duplicated wave layer Rippled wave.

The text is hard to read so let's add a white box behind it.

▶ Create a new layer and name it White background.

 ▶ Select the Rectangular Marquee Tool from the Toolbox and draw a rectangle over the text. To place the rectangle flush with the edge of the image, try and draw the rectangle so it runs over the edge of the image.

Figure 8.4

▶ Fill the rectangle with white. Make sure the white layer is under the text layer; if not, rearrange the layers in the Layers Palette.

Tip: If, when you fill the rectangle with white, only some of it is painted you are probably drawing on the **Rippled wave** layer. Be sure and select the **White background** layer before painting.

▶ Click the Horizontal Type Tool and copy the settings in Figure 8.5. Click the canvas, type Surf Club Bash, and use the Move Tool to position it on the right-hand side of the canvas (see Figure 8.7).

Figure 8.5: Type options

▷   In the Layer Styles Palette select Wow Chrome, Wow Chrome Textured.

> **Tip:** To find out the name of a style in the **Layer Styles Palette**, hover the mouse over the style and its name will pop up after a couple of seconds

▷   Click the Horizontal Type Tool again and click once below the Surf Club Bash text. Copy the settings in Figure 8.6.

Figure 8.6: Type options

▷   Type –BBQ (Enter), –Volley Ball (Enter), –Surfing competition (Enter), –Lifeguard iron man race (Enter), –Dancing and grooving until late (Enter).

▷   Select View, Grid from the Menu bar to draw a grid over your canvas. You can now use the Move Tool to align the new text with your previous text.

To highlight the activities we will add a surfboard shape backdrop.

▷   Make a new layer and call it Surfboard. Select the Elliptical Marquee Tool and draw a selection over the activities. Move it to match Figure 8.7.

▷   Colour it a dark-blue and move the layer behind the text. Experiment with layer blends on the surfboard to give different effects.

▷   Select View, Grid to take the grid away – all done! Save and close the flyer.

Figure 8.7: The finished party flyer

Montage some pictures together

We are going to montage three pictures together to make a vintage-looking artwork, then choose a title and typeface to suit it.

▶　First you need to open image 0006521.jpg from the Photoshop Elements CD, or download it from www.payne-gallway.co.uk/elements.

Figure 8.8: Image 0006521.jpg

▶　Use the Clone Stamp Tool to clone some sand over the sea shell using a bit of the broken sand ripple from above the shell. See how seamlessly you can take out the shell.

▶　Save the image as Egypt Montage, making sure it is saved with a Photoshop file format as this allows layers.

▶　Next open image 0005000.jpg from the CD, or download it from www.payne-gallway.co.uk/elements.

Figure 8.9: Image 0005000.jpg

Removing the camel's cap

For this we will use the Lasso Tool with the Clone Tool.

▶ Select the Lasso Tool, set the Feather option to 1 px and make sure the Anti-aliased box is checked.

Figure 8.10: Lasso Tool options

▶ Zoom in to make the head nice and big so that you can make an accurate selection.

▶ Reselect the Lasso Tool and draw the selection around the top of the eye to select the cap as in Figure 8.11.

Tip: When drawing selections using the **Lasso Tool**, try holding down the **Alt** key while you click and draw; this will allow you to draw straight lines.

Figure 8.11: Drawing a selection with the Lasso Tool

▶ Use a large soft Clone Stamp Tool to paint over the cap: be sure to clone the correct shade of sky.

▶ On the Menu bar click Select, Inverse.

Tip: When working on a tricky bit of selected photo retouching it is often helpful to hide the selection by pressing **Ctrl-H**.

▶ With a smaller brush, carefully take out the cap shadow on the camel's head. When you have finished, press Ctrl-D to deselect.

Copying and pasting between files

We are going to paste the camel picture into the photo of the sand.

▶ Go to the Select menu and click All, or press Ctrl-A, to select the entire canvas.

▶ Select Edit, Copy from the Menu bar.

▶ To see which images are open in Photoshop Elements select Window, Images from the Menu bar. Names of open images are listed on the menu. Click Egypt Montage to select it.

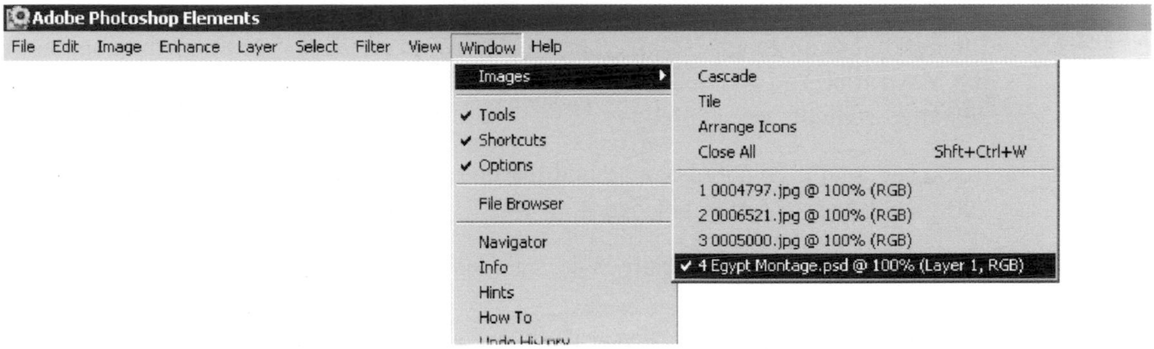

Figure 8.12: Choosing an open image from the Menu bar

▶ Now that you have the file you want in view, select Edit, Paste from the Menu bar.

▶ Change the layer blend (top left in the Layers Palette) of the camel layer to Hard Light – looks good, doesn't it?

Adding a third image

Now we'll open another image which we will then merge with the camel image.

▶ Open image 0004797.jpg from the CD, or download it from www.payne-gallway.co.uk/elements.

Figure 8.13: Image 0004797.jpg

We are going to insert the image of a compass into the picture.

▶   Select the image and paste it into the Egypt Montage.psd file, just as you did with the camel. Change the layer blend to Hard Light.

Adding extra effects and text

A great effect you can try is simply to invert the colours so white becomes black and vice versa.

▶   With the Compass layer selected, go to Image, Adjustments, Invert on the Menu bar.

▶   Change the layer blend to Colour Dodge and reduce the opacity to 30%.

▶   The next bit is up to you, so use your artistic eye to resize and position the compass with the Move Tool. You can get away with making the compass bigger because of the degraded style of the picture.

▶   If you see a light coloured box around the compass you can use the Eraser Tool with a 200 pixel brush to soften any edges.

▶   Add some text in an appropriate style, size and position - you can make up a title of your own.

Figure 8.14: Add a title of your own

Warping text

○ Double-click the Type layer thumbnail in the Layers Palette. The text should now be highlighted.

○ Now select the Create Warped Text icon located in the Options bar.

Figure 8.15: Text Options

○ Select Bulge from the Style pull-down menu. Experiment with the settings and observe how the text changes, then copy the settings in Figure 8.16. Click OK when you're done.

Figure 8.16: Warp Text options

Here's the final picture! Try merging some more photos together, experimenting with some different effects.

Figure 8.17: The picture with the warped text

Print–ready artwork

In this project we create a book cover that could be sent off to a print company for printing professionally.

When artwork is sent to print, there are certain criteria expected by printers.

Bleed

There needs to be 4mm 'bleed' (a border around the artwork just in case there is slight movement when the printed sheets are cut into the correct sizes).

Resolution

A resolution of 300 dpi is needed to ensure good image quality.

File format

The image needs to be in CMYK (Cyan, Magenta, Yellow and Black) format. In Photoshop we have been working with RGB (Red, Green, Blue) format; Photoshop Elements does not convert RGB image files to CMYK, so you would have to ask the printer to do that for you. The full version of Photoshop includes the facility to convert to CMYK for print-ready artwork.

Selecting the correct size canvas

An average size for a paperback novel is 13cm wide by 19.5cm high, and you need to add a 4mm border for the 'bleed', so the final canvas size should be 13.8 cm by 20.3 high.

▶   Open a new canvas and copy the settings in Figure 8.18.

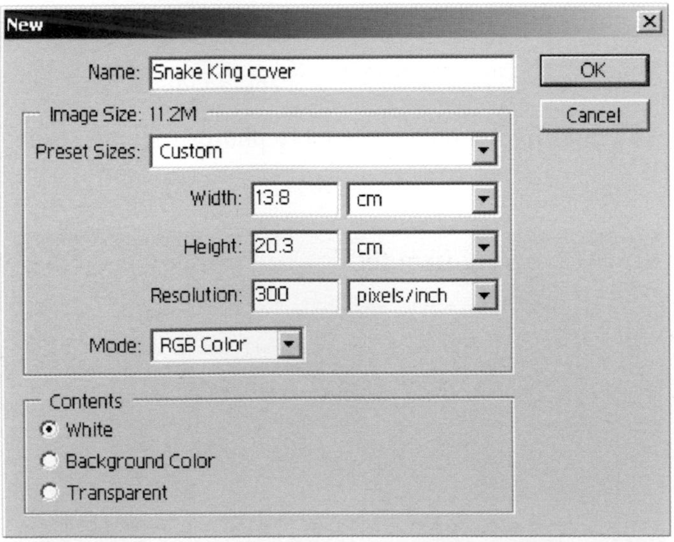

Figure 8.18: Opening a new canvas at the correct size and resolution

Creating a textured background

We are going to use different filters to make a snake skin texture.

 ● Using a large paintbrush, paint some stripes as shown in Figure 8.19.

Figure 8.19: Painted background

Note: You will notice the filters and even the paintbrush might run slowly because of the larger file size.

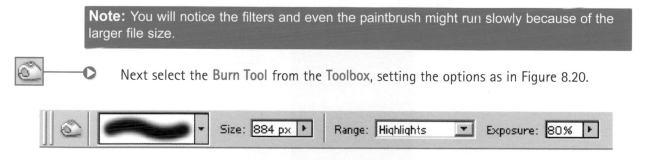

● Next select the **Burn Tool** from the **Toolbox**, setting the options as in Figure 8.20.

Figure 8.20: Burn Tool options

● Burn each side of the background to give a rounded feel – look ahead to Figure 8.25, notice that the edges of the cover are darker.

▷ Duplicate the layer and name it Stained Glass filter.

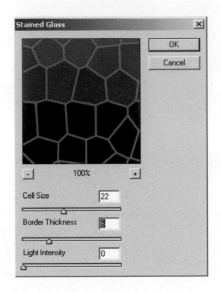

▷ The next filter uses the foreground colour so pick a medium grey foreground colour.

▷ Select Filter, Texture, Stained Glass from the Menu bar, and copy the settings in Figure 8.21. Click OK.

Figure 8.21: Stained glass filter options

▷ Duplicate the layer and name it Plastic wrap filter. Select Filter, Blur, Gaussian Blur, and set it to radius 4.6 pixels. Click OK.

▷ Select Filter, Artistic, Plastic Wrap from the Menu bar and copy the settings in Figure 8.22. Click OK.

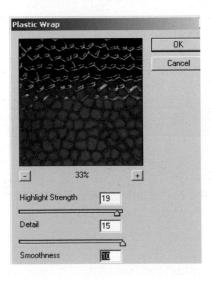

Figure 8.22: Plastic Wrap options

This looks great, but the filters are quite harsh for a background to the title of a book, so we will use the options in the Layers Palette to make the effects much more subtle. Your effects may look slightly different from mine but this does not matter.

⊙ Select the layer named Stained glass filter and drop the opacity to around 6%.

⊙ Select the Plastic wrap filter layer and drop the opacity to 60%. Change the Blend Options to Overlay.

 ⊙ Click the Type Tool and select a font; type the name of the book: Curse of the Snake King.

> **Tip:** To edit the text that you have written, select the **Type Tool** from the Toolbox, click the **Text Layer** thumbnail in the **Layers Palette** then change the settings in the **Options** bar.

Using the rulers and grid

Before you use the Move Tool to tweak the text, you can switch on some rulers and the grid to make sure you don't encroach on the bleed.

First we'll make sure the rulers are set to metric measurements.

⊙ Go to Edit, Preferences, Units & Rulers and set the rulers to cm.

⊙ Go to View, Rulers. Notice that rulers have appeared around the outside of the canvas.

⊙ Now go to View, Grid and a grid appears over the entire canvas. You should now be able to work out just how far the text needs to go.

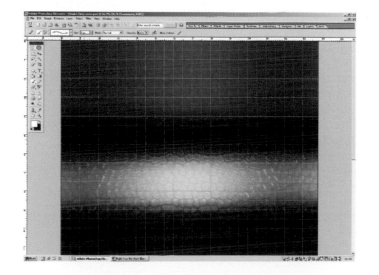

Figure 8.23: The rulers and grid are now visible

⊙ If you need to, reposition the text using the Move Tool.

⊙ Now add a Layer Style to the text layer. Select Wow Chrome Textured.

Adding a text effect

You can't use any Photoshop filters or enhancement tools on a Type layer, so you need to simplify the layer. The layer then becomes a bitmap layer and you will not be able to edit the words with the Type Tool so check your spelling now!

▷ Click to select the Type layer in the Layers Palette and select Layer, Simplify Layer from the Menu bar.

▷ Select Enhance, Adjust Colour, Hue/Saturation from the Menu bar. Copy the settings in Figure 8.24 to make the text look golden.

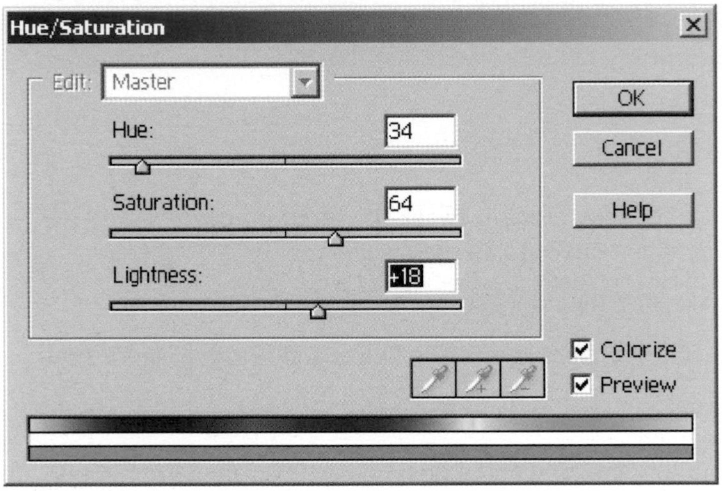

Figure 8.24: Hue/Saturation dialogue box

▷ Write a fake review and place it along the bottom of the cover. Size it, being careful not to go into the bleed.

▷ Right-click the Type layer containing the review in the Layers Palette and select Simplify Layer from the shortcut menu that appears.

▷ Select Filter, Distort, Ripple from the Menu bar. Set the Amount to -75 and the Size to Large. Click OK.

▷ If you want to change the colour or lighten or darken the text select Enhance, Adjust Color, Hue/Saturation from the Menu bar.

▷ You can now add a Layer Style on your new ripple text if you want – I added a drop shadow.

The finished cover: A magnificent bestseller!

Figure 8.25: The finished cover

Fixing Problems with Photos

This chapter focuses on various problems that arise with photos and scanned images. We'll go through how to remove red eye and how to patch up damaged photos. There is also a section on scanning, with an explanation of the various settings along with problem solving tips. Finally we'll have some fun creating a panoramic image out of a set of photos.

You will need a picture of a friend with a bad case of red eye; or you can download the photo I've used from www.payne-gallway.co.uk/elements.

▶ Open Photoshop Elements and select File, Open from the Menu bar. Open Bill.jpg or open your own red eye photo.

Figure 9.1: A photo with red eye

Rotating and adjusting the image

Before we get rid of the red eye we need to rotate the image; we will also have a play with some image settings.

We can rotate the image in several ways:

○ Select Image, Rotate, 90° Right from the Menu bar. Now click the Step Backward icon so we can experiment with another way of rotating photos.

○ There is a great feature in Elements for quickly sorting out your photos. Select Enhance, Quick Fix from the Menu bar.

The Quick Fix window will open as shown in Figure 9.2.

Figure 9.2: The Quick Fix window

This window will allow you to make lots of small changes to enhance your picture.

○ Check the Rotate option box (bottom left) and select Rotate 90° Right. Now click Apply.

You will notice the After screen is now showing Bill the right way up.

○ On the right-hand side of the window is the Undo button, click this to undo the previous operation. Click the Redo button to redo the rotation.

○ Now select Brightness, then choose Auto Contrast. If it improves your image then keep it, and if not click Undo.

○ The Focus option will allow you to either Auto Focus (sharpen) or Blur your photo; you will need to experiment to see which helps. In the case of the photo of Bill, I would Blur it because this will help lose some of the graininess in the photo.

○ Click OK when you're done.

Removing red eye

Red eye happens when the camera flash reflects back from the back of the eye; it is quite common but very easy to fix.

○ Click the Red Eye Brush Tool in the Toolbox (7th spot down on the right) and change the red eye options to match Figure 9.3.

The **Current** window will show the colour that is going to be replaced.

Click on **Replacement** and select a very dark blue to match Bill's eyes.

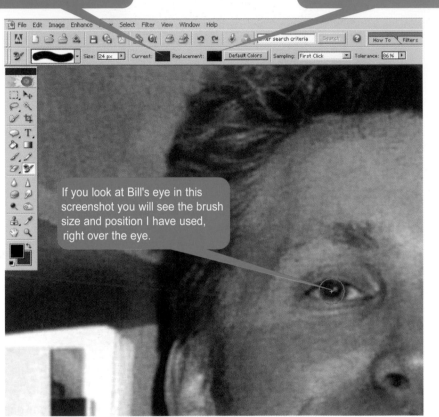

If you look at Bill's eye in this screenshot you will see the brush size and position I have used, right over the eye.

Figure 9.3: Red eye options

○ Click the eye and hey presto! The red eye disappears. You may need to play with the Tolerance if the entire red eye is not fixed.

○ Now redo the process for the other eye.

Tip: If the person in the photo has very red skin the red eye brush might try to change the skin tone as well; lower the tolerance to stop this.

Figure 9.4: Red eye fixed

Applying a filter

Just for fun let's apply a filter to make the photo look like a brilliant pencil sketch.

○ Select Filter, Brush Strokes, Cross Hatch from the Menu bar. Copy the settings in Figure 9.5 then click OK.

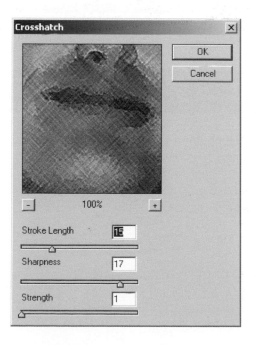

Figure 9.5: Cross hatch filter

Add a photo frame

To finish off let's add a photo frame.

▶   Click the Effects tab in the Palette Well then select Frames from the pull-down menu. Choose a frame you like – I went for the Photo Corner effect.

Figure 9.6: Add a photo frame

Tip: You will notice that the frame is automatically added onto its own layer, so you have the option to switch it on and off.

▶   Save and close the photo. If you don't want to overwrite the original, save it under a different file name.

Scratched and dusty old photos

For this you will need an aged or damaged photo; if you don't have your own you can download this photo from www.payne-gallway.co.uk/elements.

Figure 9.7: Damaged photo

▶ Open the image Stuart.jpg.

▶ Select Filter, Dust & Scratches from the Menu bar. Using Figure 9.8 as a starting point, try changing the Radius and Threshold values to improve the photograph. See if you can make it better than mine. The aim is to get rid of the unwanted marks without making the photo too blurred.

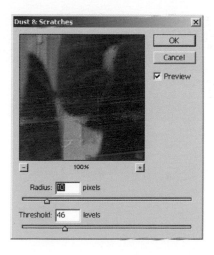

Figure 9.8: Dust and Scratches filter

▶ Click OK when you are done.

▶ The photo is very faded. Open the Quick Fix window (on the Enhance menu) and make some changes. (I found Auto Contrast helped.)

▶ On really bad photos like this one you will need to use the Clone Stamp Tool to fix some problems. See how good you can make it.

▶ Lastly, use the Rectangle Marquee Tool to draw a square just inside the white frame of the photo; try and get it as accurate as possible. Select Selection, Inverse from the Menu bar then paint the selection white. This will create a new white border.

Figure 9.9: Finished job!

Crop Marks

If you are printing something at home that will need to be cut to size, it is useful to add crop marks to mark out the exact size you need to cut to. The photo we have just edited has a white border so when you print it you won't know exactly where the border ends; we will add some crop marks to show where the corners of the photo are.

○ Select File, Print Preview from the Menu bar.

○ In the bottom left of the Print Preview window is a check box called Show More Options. Check this.

○ Make sure Output is selected in the drop-down list. Now check the box marked Corner Crop Marks.

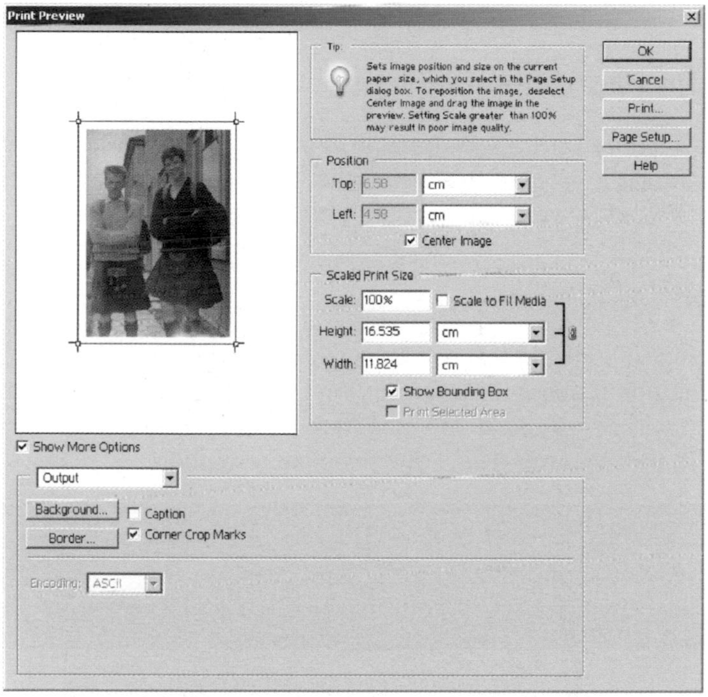

Figure 9.10: Print Preview with crop marks

○ Either click Print to print the photo with crop marks, or click OK to close Print Preview without printing.

○ Save and close the touched-up photo.

> **Tip:** Professional printers use crop marks, but you would never send an image to a printer with crop marks on because the printer would always add their own.

Print Screen

If you ever want to literally take a picture of your entire screen, you can use the Print Screen function. You might use this to take a picture of a website.

It doesn't matter if you have Elements running or not, just press the Print Screen key on your keyboard (probably named Prt Scr), usually at the top of your keyboard. Open Photoshop Elements if it is not already open. When you look in File you will see an option New from Clipboard. Click it and the screen grab will appear. You can crop it or change it like any other raster image.

Top tips for scanning!

Each scanner comes with different scanning software but all scanners will have the main features in common.

Starting a scan from Photoshop Elements

You should be able to start a scan through Photoshop by selecting File, Import from the Menu bar. If your scanner is listed in this menu, click to select it and follow the onscreen instructions. Some makes of scanner aren't compatible with this and may not appear on the menu.

Scanning resolution

If you are going to print the scanned image at the same size as it was scanned, a good scanning resolution is about 300dpi. Your printer probably won't print at higher resolutions than this so it will be wasted. If you plan to reduce the image in size or you don't need a good quality picture then you can reduce the scanning resolution.

> **Tip**: Don't use a higher resolution than you need to because it will take longer to scan and create a huge file!
> If the scanning resolution is too low the picture will look pixelated, especially if you enlarge it.

Black and white pictures

If you are going to print out your scanned images on a black and white printer, or the images you are scanning are black and white, scan them in greyscale mode. This is faster to scan and the file size is smaller.

> **Tip:** You can scan 3D items such as a pencil; just put a large blanket or coat over the scanner to cut out the light.

Images larger than A4

You can scan large items in several sections and piece them together in Photoshop Elements. You could try using the Photomerge function for this – we cover that later on.

Fixing moiré on scanned images

When you scan a printed document, such as a book cover or a page in a magazine, you will get a strange pattern on your scan; this pattern is called Moiré. Moiré is worse at lower scanning resolutions, but can still be present even at high resolutions. Be aware that the moiré will look much worse when you print the image than it will on screen.

> **Tip:** Remember that in most cases, scanning print is a copyright infringement, so be careful not to use copyrighted images without permission.

We'll run through how to get rid of some of the moiré here.

▶ You will need a scan with a bad case of moiré. If you don't have one, download the image in Figure 9.11 from www.payne-gallway.co.uk/elements.

Notice the strange check pattern that appears on the scan; this is called moiré. The pattern was not present on the scanned book cover.

Figure 9.11: A scanned book cover with moiré

▶ Open the image. Use the Zoom Tool to zoom in so you can see the moiré pattern.

This will look 200% worse in print than it looks on screen. We can get rid of it, or at least make it better, by using a filter.

The Despeckle filter

▶   Select Filter, Noise, Despeckle from the Menu bar.

Figure 9.12: The Despeckle filter reduces the moiré

Notice that the moiré has reduced a little. We will keep applying the filter until the pattern is gone.

▶   Select Filter from the Menu bar; notice that the Despeckle option has been added to the top of the Filter menu for convenience. Click it to apply it again. Keep applying the Despeckle filter until the pattern has gone.

Tip: To reapply the filter you have just used, just press **Ctrl-F**.

The image has degraded really badly, so we'll try a different filter.

▶   Select File, Revert from the Menu bar; this will take you back to the last saved version of the file.

The Median filter

Tip: The **Median** filter is better than the **Despeckle** filter because it doesn't blur the image as much.

◗ This time, use the Despeckle filter just once to reduce some of the pattern without degrading the image.

◗ Select Filter, Noise, Median from the Menu bar. Copy the settings in Figure 9.13. Use the image preview to judge how much to use the filter before the image starts breaking up.

Tip: If you rescan the image at several different resolutions you may find one that shows hardly any moiré at all.

Figure 9.13: The Median filter window

◗ You may need to apply the Median filter once more. Be careful not to damage the scan too much.

◗ Save and close the improved image.

Create a panoramic image

This is great fun. We've all got a set of holiday panoramic photos showing the view from the hotel window; now you can merge them all together professionally! To do this we will use the Photomerge function.

▷   You will need a set of photos that were shot consecutively into a panorama. If you don't have one, just download the images from www.payne-gallway.co.uk/elements.

▷   Select File, Create Photomerge from the Menu bar. The Photomerge window appears.

Selecting the photos

First you need to select which images you want to merge.

▷   Click the Browse button and navigate to the folder with your photos. You can select all the photos at once by holding down the Shift key while you click the first and last file names.

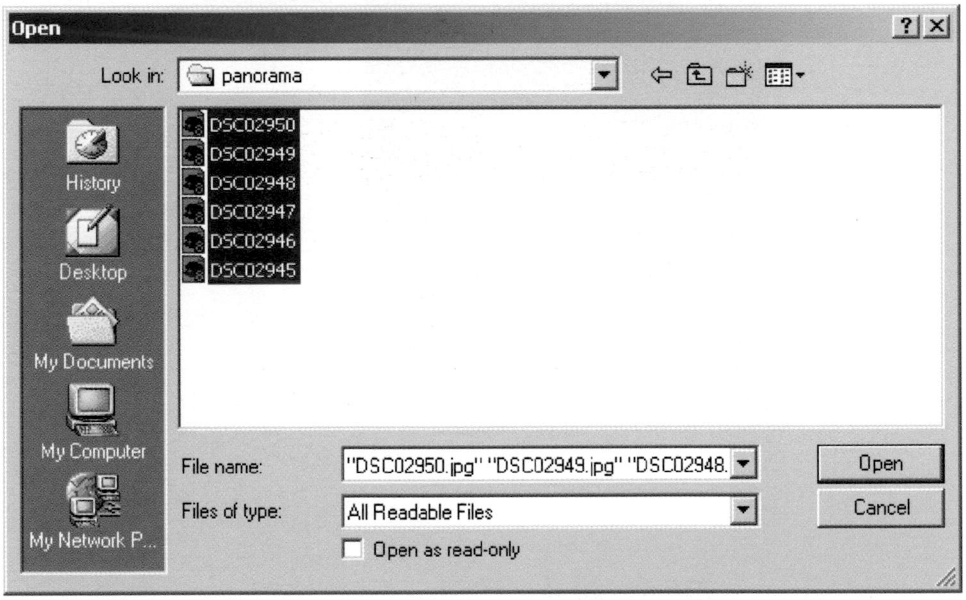

Figure 9.14: Selecting files for the photomerge.

Merging the photos

◑ Click Open, then click OK in the Photomerge window.

You will have to wait a little while whilst Elements tries to automatically put the scene together. If it doesn't match the photos correctly, follow the next set of instructions. It's very easy!

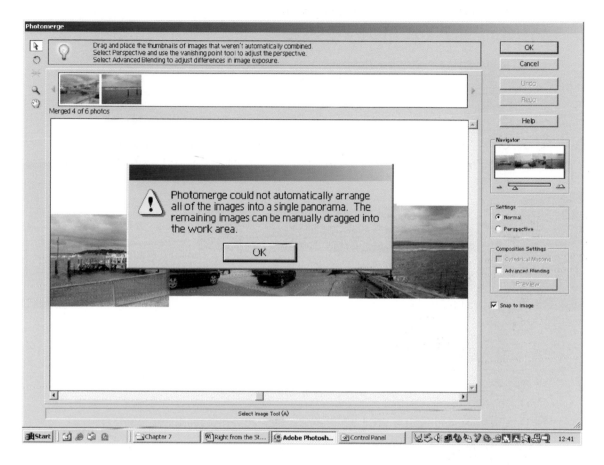

Figure 9.15: The Photomerge window

◑ Click OK in the dialogue box that appears.

◑ Make sure the options match the right-hand side of Figure 9.15.

◑ Click the Select Image Tool in the top left of the Photomerge window.

Repositioning the photos

◐   All you need do to rearrange the images is click and drag them. You can put some of the photos in the smaller white box at the top of the window to get them out of the way while you arrange others. When you drag one image over another, drag it as near as you can to where you think it should go, and when you release the mouse Photoshop will exactly match the photos for you! Clever eh?

Your screen should now look like Figure 9.16.

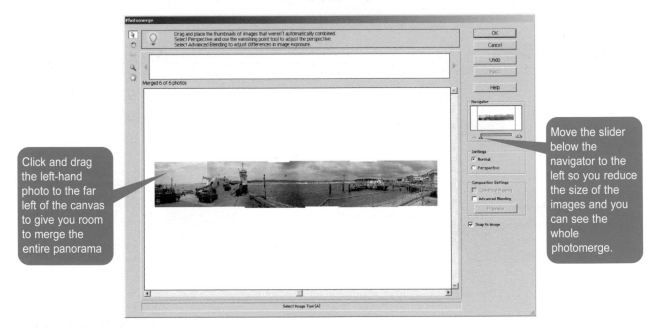

Click and drag the left-hand photo to the far left of the canvas to give you room to merge the entire panorama

Move the slider below the navigator to the left so you reduce the size of the images and you can see the whole photomerge.

Figure 9.16: Complete Photomerge

◐   Click OK, and wait a little while whilst Elements merges them together.

When Elements has merged the photos, the photomerge will appear on the canvas as a new image.

Tidying up the image

Now we'll neaten the edges.

◉ Select the Crop Tool and draw a square over the photomerge. Move the nodes so you don't have any transparent bits showing. Click the Commit current crop operation icon.

Figure 9.17: Crop the rough edges

◉ Save the image as Panorama photomerge.psd then close it.

Tip: The shortcut to close an image is **Ctrl-W**.

Adding perspective

Now we'll look at recreating the panorama with added perspective.

◉ Select File, Photomerge from the Menu bar. Select the same photos as before and click OK.

◉ Rearrange the photos if you need to. This time, on the right of the Photomerge window, under Settings, click to select Perspective.

◉ Save it as Panorama photomerge perspective.psd.

Figure 9.18: Photomerge with perspective added.

Retouching

Choose which of the two panoramic images you prefer because now you're going to retouch one.

▶ Use the Clone Stamp Tool and the Dodge Tool to get rid of the dark lines and match the clouds more realistically.

▶ Use a Lens Flare (Filter, Render, Lens Flare) to add some dramatics.

The finished panorama

Figure 9.19: A few minutes of retouching

Cut-outs and Painting Selections

10

One of the bread and butter jobs for a freelance illustrator is Cut-Outs; generally this involves taking a photo of a product and very neatly cutting it out and placing it on a different background.

Here are two exercises showing different techniques to do a quick and neat job. There's also some added fun with filters at the end of the chapter.

Create a bit of Holland

In this project we will cut out some tulips and paste them onto a windmill photo. We will use the Selection Brush Tool, a real help in cutting out images and making complicated selections.

▶ Open image 0006546.jpg from the Elements CD, or download it from www.payne-gallway.co.uk/elements.

Cutting out the tulips

▶ Click the Magic Wand Tool and set the tolerance level to 60. Click the red background. Experiment with setting the tolerance level.

Figure 10.1: Messy selection

The darker colours at the bottom of the tulips are making things a bit messy. We'll need to try something else.

▷ Undo the selection by clicking **Ctrl-D**.

▷ Click the red background just once with the **Magic Wand Tool** with tolerance **60**. This is messy, but it is a useful starting point.

▷ Click the **Selection Brush Tool** and copy the settings in Figure 10.2 to the **Options** bar. You will notice the areas that are not selected have turned blue (or whichever you have selected as the **Overlay Color** in the **Options bar**); this is like a plastic mask that you can add to or take away.

> If you would prefer another mask colour, click on the **Overlay Color** and change the colour in the palette.

Figure 10.2: Selection Brush Tool options in the Options bar

◉ Go to Select, Inverse on the Menu bar. This inverses the current selection.

◉ Using suitable brush sizes, paint around the edges of the tulips. Use the Zoom Tool and the Step Backward icon to get a really accurate selection. Use Figure 10.3 as a guide.

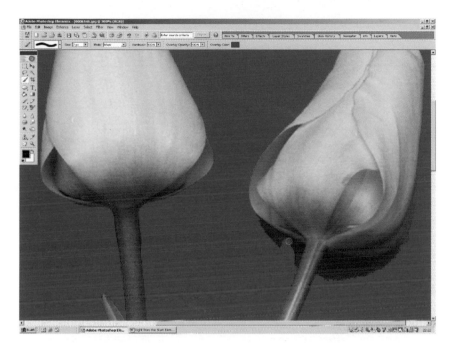

Figure 10.3: Selection Brush painting around the tulip

◉ With the Selection Brush Tool, change the Mode setting in the Options bar to Selection.

> **Tip:** Use the **Shift** key to draw straight lines with the **Selection Brush Tool.** Press and hold **Shift** then click the left mouse button where you want the line to end. You can paint very accurately around the edges like this.

◉ Save the image as Tulip selection.psd and leave it open. If your image has been maximized so that it takes up the whole Photoshop screen, click the Maximise/Minimise icon on the top right of the image to make it smaller.

Preparing the new background image

▷   Open image 0006614.jpg from the Elements CD, or download it from www.payne-gallway.co.uk/elements.

Now brighten up the image:

▷   Select Enhance, Adjust Brightness/Contrast, Brightness/Contrast from the Menu bar and copy the settings from Figure 10.4.

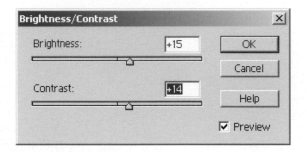

Figure 10.4: The Brightness/Contrast window

▷   Click OK. Now arrange the two images like Figure 10.5.

Figure 10.5: Arranging the image windows

Pasting a selection onto a new background

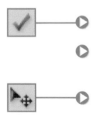 With the tulip picture at the front (just click on the canvas if it is not) click the Move Tool then click and drag the tulips onto the windmill image. Make sure you click within the selection, or the whole image will be moved – we only want the selection.

Size the tulips so they look like Figure 10.6.

Figure 10.6: Tulips sized in the windmill image

Click the Commit Transform icon to complete the resize.

Look in the Layers Palette; there is now a new layer containing your tulips. Duplicate the layer twice; name the layers yellow tulip, orange tulip and pink tulip.

Click on the layer thumbnail for the orange tulip layer, then use the Move Tool to move it away from behind the other tulips. Repeat this for the pink tulip layer.

Changing the colour of the tulips

○   Click the orange tulip layer then select Enhance, Adjust Color, Replace Color.

 ○   The cursor becomes an eyedropper icon; click in the center of the yellow tulip then copy the settings in Figure 10.7.

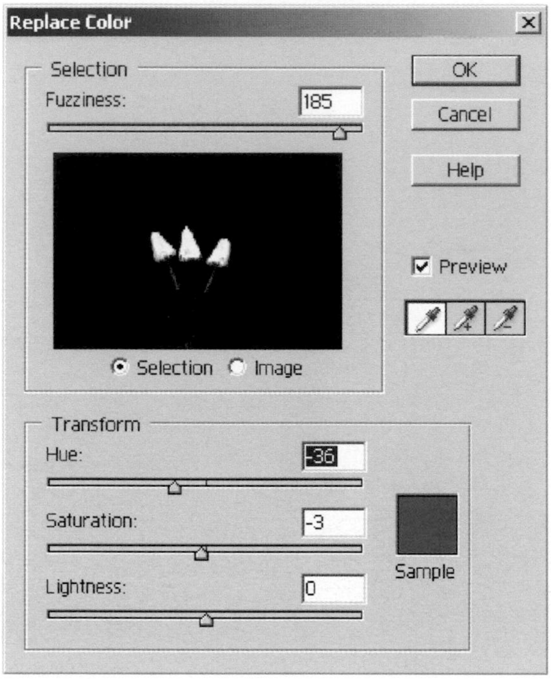

Figure 10.7: Replace Colour Window

○   Look at the preview; if you find that the yellow hasn't completely disappeared, try increasing the Fuzziness value at the top of the Replace Colour window.

○   When you're happy with the colour of the tulip, click OK.

The orange tulip layer now contains orange tulips!

○   Click the pink tulip layer. Repeat what you did above with the Replace Colour window; this time change the Hue value to a pink colour.

Duplicating a selection onto the same layer

 ○   Select the Move Tool.

○   We now have tulips of three different colours. In the Layers Palette click the pink tulip layer to select it. Now hold down the Ctrl key and wave the curser icon over the selected layer in the Layers Palette; a little square marquee will appear. Click the layer.

 ○   Look at the canvas; your tulip has been selected. Move the curser over the tulip on your canvas. Hold down the Ctrl and Alt keys and when you see the double arrow icon, click and drag to make a new copy of the tulip. Repeat this to make a few more.

Duplicating a selection onto a different layer

Notice that each new pink tulip is being placed on the pink tulip layer. We'll use a different method to duplicate the orange tulips just to show you the difference.

○ Deselect (Ctrl-D) and click the orange tulip layer in the Layers Palette. This time hold down the Ctrl and Alt keys and click and drag the tulips to make a few copies.

Look in the Layers Palette and you will see that each duplicated tulip has been put on a different layer. We actually want them on one layer. It's a bad idea to use more layers than you need because they dramatically increase the file size.

Merging layers

We'll merge the orange tulip layers now.

○ Make sure you have the highest orange tulip layer selected in the Layers Palette. Click the More button in the top right of the Layers Palette and select Merge Down.

○ Merge Down again until you are back to your original orange tulip layer.

○ Click to select the yellow tulip layer; duplicate this on the same layer, as you did for the pink tulips.

Figure 10.8: The finished artwork!

Good cut-outs look really effective.

○ Save the image as Tulips with windmill.psd then close it. Close the original tulip image if it is still open.

Bear necessities

There is one more tool, the Magic Eraser Tool, that is great for quick cut-outs especially when you have a complicated shape.

▶ Open image 0004878.jpg from the Elements CD, or download it from www.payne-gallway.co.uk/elements.

Making the bear background transparent

To do this we will use the Eraser Tool and the Magic Eraser Tool.

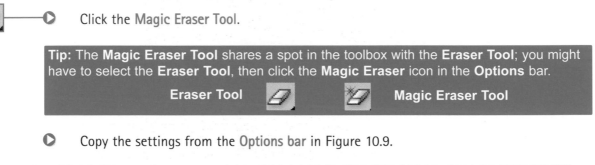 ▶ Click the Magic Eraser Tool.

Tip: The **Magic Eraser Tool** shares a spot in the toolbox with the **Eraser Tool**; you might have to select the **Eraser Tool**, then click the **Magic Eraser** icon in the **Options** bar.

Eraser Tool   **Magic Eraser Tool**

▶ Copy the settings from the Options bar in Figure 10.9.

Figure 10.9: Magic Eraser Tool options in the Options bar

▶ Click repeatedly on the background of the bear. Make sure you don't delete the tree, we need that!

Click the background. You will still have to do a certain amount of tidying up, but this will get rid of most of the background.

Figure 10.10: Deleting the background

Use the Eraser Tool in the Options bar to delete the last little bits. Change the eraser size if you need to.

Figure 10.11: Cut-out bear.

The edges are very rough so we can use the Smudge Tool to create a realistic fur effect.

Select the Smudge Tool from the Toolbox then find the Spatter Brush in the Options bar. Copy the rest of the settings in Figure 10.12.

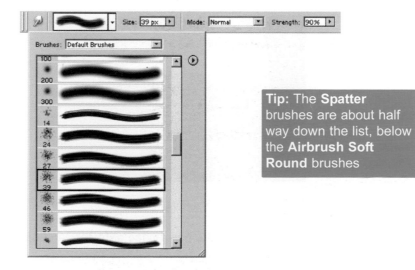

Tip: The **Spatter** brushes are about half way down the list, below the **Airbrush Soft Round** brushes

Figure 10.12. Smudge Tool options

Smudge the edges around the bear. To get a really good fur effect, click near the edge of the outline and drag away to create wisps of hair! Use the Zoom Tool if you need to.

Figure 10.13: Hairy edge created using the Smudge Tool

Save the bear as Bear transparent background.psd.

Note: If we saved the file as a **JPEG** file, Elements would add a white background instead of the transparent background, because **JPEG** files do not support transparent backgrounds.

Pasting the bear on a new background

Now we'll open an image onto which we'll paste the bear.

Open 0006723.jpg from the Elements CD, or download it from www.payne-gallway.co.uk/elements.

Figure 10.14: Image 0006723.jpg

Click the Move Tool and drag the bear image onto the farm background, just like you did the tulips onto the windmill background.

Reduce the size of the bear so the tree stump is only slightly larger than the height of the farm image. Press the Enter key to Commit Transform.

Tip: When transforming images press the **Shift** key to keep the proportions of the image.

Changing the light source and colour

If we look at the two images the light sources are different. Also, the light in the farm background is warm and yellowy whereas the bear has quite a cold light. We'll fix both these problems now.

○ To fix the light sources the bear needs to change direction. Select Image, Rotate, Flip Layer Horizontal from the Menu bar.

○ Position the tree on the far left-hand side; don't forget to click the Commit Transform icon when you've finished the move.

○ Now select Enhance, Adjust Color, Color variations from the Menu bar. Copy the settings in Figure 10.15 to make the bear look as if he has matching warm light on him. You'll need to click the Decrease Blue button to make the bear more yellowy.

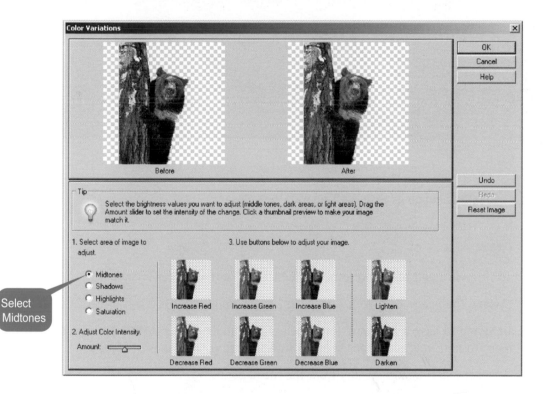

Figure 10.15: The Colour Variations window

○ Click OK when you're happy with the settings.

Much more realistic!

Figure 10.16: Finished! The bear is on the farm!

▶   Save this image as Bear on farm.psd, then close it.

The Liquify filter

Just for fun we'll add some interesting effects to our cut-out bear image.

▶   Open the image Bear with transparent background.psd if it is not already open.

We are going to have a look at a very special filter hidden in the Distort options. Your friends will learn to hate you as humans seem to suffer worst at the hands of Liquify!

▶   Select Filter, Distort, Liquify from the Menu bar.

There are quite a few options in this filter – they are listed on the left of the Liquify window. Here's a brief run-through what they all do:

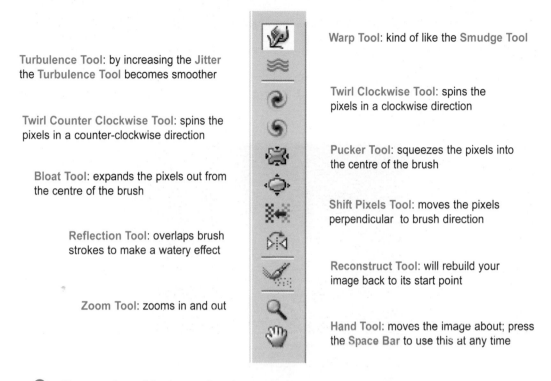

Turbulence Tool: by increasing the Jitter the Turbulence Tool becomes smoother

Twirl Counter Clockwise Tool: spins the pixels in a counter-clockwise direction

Bloat Tool: expands the pixels out from the centre of the brush

Reflection Tool: overlaps brush strokes to make a watery effect

Zoom Tool: zooms in and out

Warp Tool: kind of like the Smudge Tool

Twirl Clockwise Tool: spins the pixels in a clockwise direction

Pucker Tool: squeezes the pixels into the centre of the brush

Shift Pixels Tool: moves the pixels perpendicular to brush direction

Reconstruct Tool: will rebuild your image back to its start point

Hand Tool: moves the image about; press the Space Bar to use this at any time

▶ Have a play with the settings!

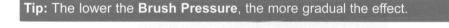

Tip: The lower the **Brush Pressure**, the more gradual the effect.

Figure 10.17: The Liquify filter creates a very strange beastie!

▶ Click OK when you're done.

Neon Lights filter

We'll add one more effect to our bear.

▶   Select Layer, Flatten Image from the Menu bar.

This adds a white background where it was previously transparent.

▶   In the Palette Well click the Effects tab to open the Effects Palette. Make sure All is selected in the drop-down list at the top of the palette; find the Neon Lights filter and double-click it. Even weirder eh?

Figure 10.18: The Neon Lights filter

▶   Use the Undo History Palette to undo so you have a transparent background. Duplicate the layer then create your own background for your alien bear.

Animation

11

Photoshop Elements has a great way of creating animations. Once saved they can simply be pasted into documents and web pages in the same way as images.

As with any animation, we need to create the illusion of movement by displaying a sequence of images one after the other. The animations we will create are called animated GIFs – this refers to the file format in which they are saved. Animated GIFs are created as frames, each in a separate layer. When the layered file is saved, Elements will put it together as an animation.

Creating a shape to animate

First we'll find a butterfly shape using the Custom Shapes Tool.

   ◗   Open a new canvas, 200 x 200 pixels with a white background in RGB.

   ◗   Select the Shape Selection Tool from the Toolbox (fourth spot down on the left) then click the Custom Shapes Tool in the Options bar.

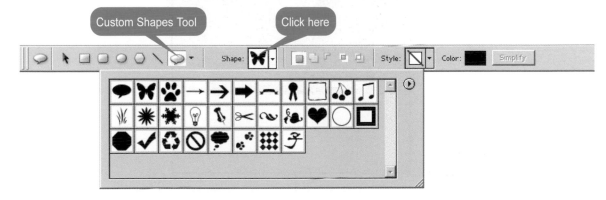

Figure 11.1: The Options bar

   ◗   Click the small down-arrow to browse all the shapes. Take a look at all the shapes available, and find the butterfly shape. Click once to select the butterfly.

Draw the butterfly on the canvas by clicking in the top left corner and dragging it across the canvas. If you're not happy with the shape, either undo and try again, or use the Move Tool to adjust it.

Figure 11.2: Draw a butterfly shape with the Custom Shapes Tool

Now apply a layer style using the Layer Styles Palette. I chose Wow Plastic Green.

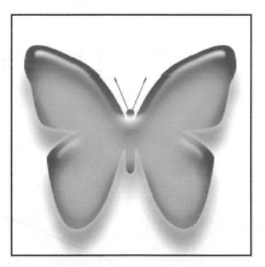

Figure 11.3: Butterfly

Adding a new layer for each frame

Now we need to duplicate this layer a couple of times, changing it slightly each time to create the frames in the animation.

Right-click the butterfly layer in the Layers Palette and select Duplicate Layer from the shortcut menu that appears.

With the Move Tool selected, tickle the left and right nodes in, then very slightly move the top and bottom nodes in. Don't use the corner nodes for this, just the ones in the middle of the sides. We want to give our butterfly a realistic flutter; look at Figure 11.4 for reference.

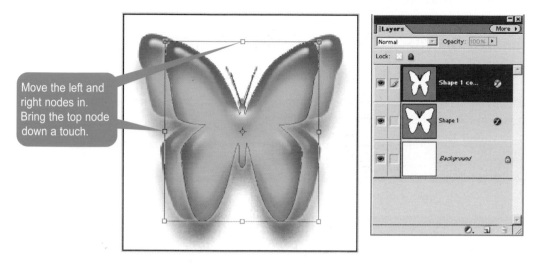

Move the left and right nodes in. Bring the top node down a touch.

Figure 11.4: Tickle the butterfly wings in

Duplicate the layer again and move the nodes even closer. Your image should now look like Figure 11.5.

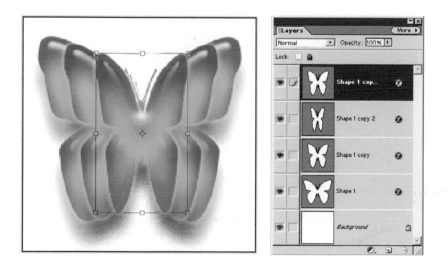

Figure 11.5

Lastly duplicate Shape 1 copy and move it to the top of the Layers Palette; this will make the butterfly animation loop.

Notice that there is a blank layer called Background in the Layers Palette. We need to delete this layer or there will be a blank frame in our animation.

▶ Right-click the Background layer and select Delete Layer from the menu that appears.

▶ Save the image as Butterfly animation images.psd.

Creating an animated GIF file

Now we'll create an animated GIF file from our layered image.

▶ Select File, Save for Web from the Menu bar. The Save for Web window appears as shown in Figure 11.6; copy the settings carefully.

Tip: You can open the **Save For web** window by clicking the **Save for Web** icon on the **Shortcuts bar**.

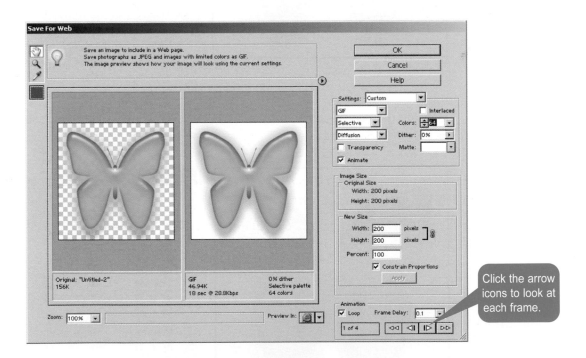

Figure 11.6: Save for Web window

▶ At the bottom-right of the Save for Web window is a Preview icon – click it so see your butterfly fly!

▶ If you don't like the frame rate, change it then press the Preview icon again.

Tip: It is possible that if you change the frame rate and then click **Preview** again, the preview will get stuck as a minimised window. If this happens, close **Internet Explorer** and the **Save for Web** window, then re-open the **Save for Web** window from the **File** menu.

▷   When you're happy with it click OK. The Save Optimised As window should appear:

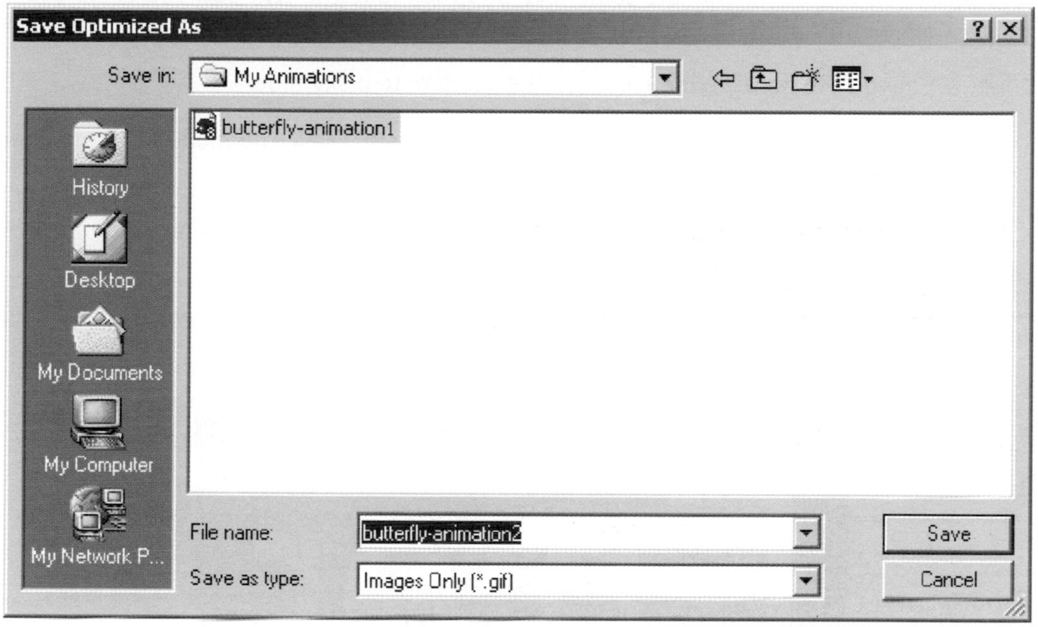

Figure 11.7: The Save window

▷   Save the animation as Butterfly-animation, and make sure the Save As Type box says Images Only (*.gif). Click Save.

Now that you have control of your animation, go back and move the nodes about to see if you can make the butterfly move more realistically.

▷   Save and close the image. You might also need to close Internet Explorer – your butterfly is probably still flying!

Animated text

In this exercise we will animate some text, and then fade the text out. You could use this as a nice simple entry into your website.

○ Change the background colour in the Toolbox to a sky blue.

○ Open a new canvas 400 pixels wide and 200 high. Make the mode RGB and change the Contents to Background Color. Click OK.

To make the text size and position perfect we will do this part of the animation in reverse then swap the layers around afterwards.

○ Write Enter in the middle of the canvas. Choose a typeface and colour you like and use the Move Tool to position and tweak it.

Figure 11.8

Adding a new layer for each frame

Look at Figure 11.9. We need to produce each layer with one character less than the previous layer.

○ Duplicate the Enter layer, then with the Type Tool selected click at the end of the text and press the Backspace key to delete it. Repeat this until you are left with just E. As you duplicate the layers, hide the other layers so you can see what is going on.

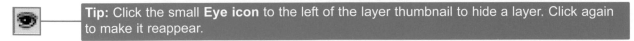

Tip: Click the small **Eye icon** to the left of the layer thumbnail to hide a layer. Click again to make it reappear.

◗ Swap the order of the layers so the Enter layer is on top.

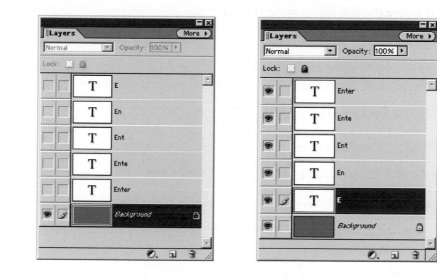

Figure 11.9: Swap layer order

Nearly there – we now have the word Enter being spelt out, and to finish we will make it fade out. We'll use the opacity settings to fade out the layer.

◗ The top layer has the entire word on it; duplicate the layer then drop the opacity to 70. Duplicate it again and drop it to 50, then another to 20.

Figure 11.10: Final layer order

◗ Make sure all the layers are visible; if any are hidden the animation will have blank frames.

Turning layers into frames for animation

Now we'll create the GIF file.

▷   Select File, Save for Web.

▷   Click the Eyedropper Tool in the top left of the Save for Web window. Click the blue background of the canvas.

▷   Click the Animate checkbox.

▷   Change the Colours to 8.

▷   In the Matte drop-down list select Eyedropper Color.

▷   Click the Loop checkbox.

▷   Change the Frame Delay to 0.1.

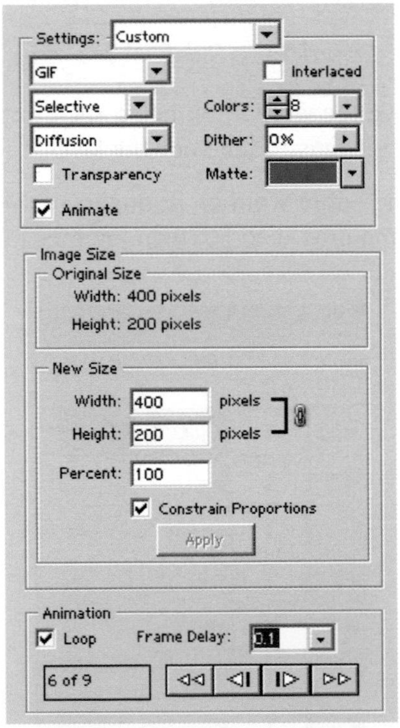

Figure 11.11: The settings in the Save for Web window

○ Check the file size of the GIF file shown below the right-hand image in the Save for Web window; mine is less than 9k – tiny!

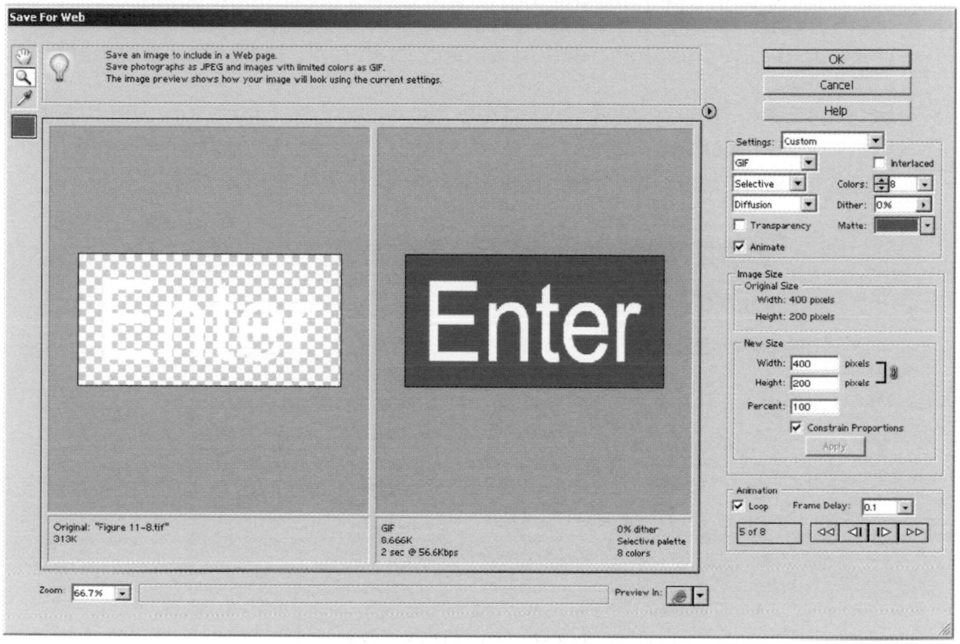

Figure 11.12: Save for Web Window

○ Preview the animation by clicking the Preview icon at the bottom right of the window. Looks pretty professional, doesn't it?

○ Click OK. Save the animation as Text-animation.gif.

○ In addition to saving the animation, you need to save the image too. Select File, Save from the Menu bar. Save the image as Text animation image.psd.

○ Close the image.

Animated panorama

We are now going to animate our photomerged panorama. We will have to save it as a GIF so the image quality won't be fantastic, but it will give a great impression.

▶ Open your saved photomerged panorama, preferably the one you retouched.

▶ Select Image, Resize, Image Size, from the Menu bar. Make sure the Resample Image and Constrain Proportions boxes are ticked (also Bicubic should be selected from the drop-down list) and make the height 300 pixels. Click OK.

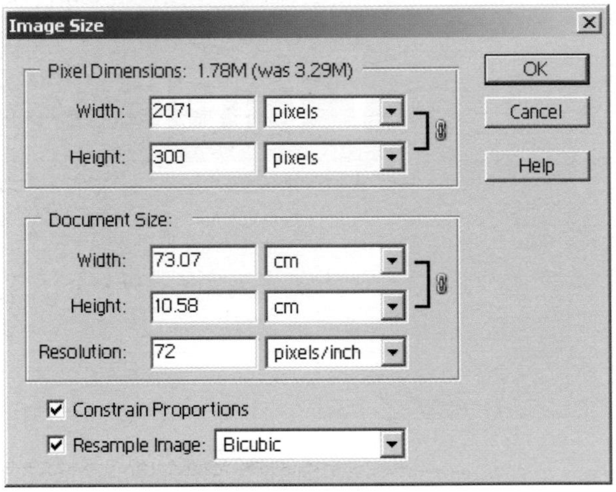

Figure 11.13: The Image Size window

▶ Go to Select, All on the Menu bar. Now select Edit, Copy.

The animation image will be much narrower than the panoramic image. We are going to paste the animation image onto the smaller canvas, then use different parts of the panorama for each layer.

▶ Open a new canvas, 300 pixels high by 400 wide, RGB Color. Specify the Contents as Transparent. Name the image Panorama animation and click OK.

▶ Select Edit, Paste from the Menu bar.

We now have the photomerged picture in our canvas.

Figure 11.14

 Duplicate the layer. Use the Move Tool to move the image to the left; you need to move it about 1/3 of the way across the canvas. Hold down the Shift key while you move it to help constrain it from moving up and down.

Duplicate the new layer and move it again. Repeat this until you get to the end of your image. I used 11 layers (so I'd have 11 frames in my animation).

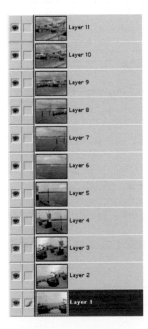

Tip: You can use the **Layer Thumbnails** as a quick guide to see how your animation is going to look.

Figure 11.15: Look at the Layer Thumbnails in the Layers Palette

Note: The more frames you add the smoother the animation, but every frame increases the file size. If you are going to use the image only on your computer you can afford to have a large file size; we will save a smaller version for the web later.

▶   Select File, Save for Web from the Menu bar.

Figure 11.16: The Save for Web window

▶   Click the Animate checkbox.

▶   If you want the image to loop, check the Loop option.

▶   Choose 256 Colors; if you drop the colour rate down and you see the image degrade badly, set Dither to 100%. This puts a noise filter over the image which should make it look a bit better.

▶   You will need a Frame Delay of 0.5.

▶   Check the File Size; it's pretty big but we can reduce it later if we need to.

▶   Click the Preview icon to see it in your browser. It'll take a few seconds to load.

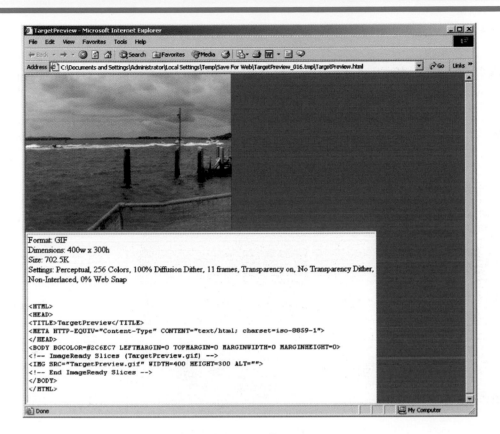

Figure 11.17: The animation in the browser window

Tip: Use the **Stop** and **Refresh** icons in your browser window to stop and replay the animation.

Isn't that great! It looks like you're panning round with a video camera! Try repeating this exercise with a panoramic photo that actually meets at the ends i.e. it spans 360°. That would make a brilliant looped animation.

▶ Change the settings in the Save for Web window if you want to, otherwise click OK and save the animation as Panoramic animation.gif.

Reducing the file size

We can make a low resolution web version and dramatically reduce the file size; it will still be a relatively big file for the web but you could give people the choice of whether or not to download it. We will change the image size using the Save for Web window.

Apply ─► Select File, Save for Web. Change the image Height to 150 pixels then click Apply. Use all the settings as before but reduce the colours to 128; you will see the file size has almost quartered.

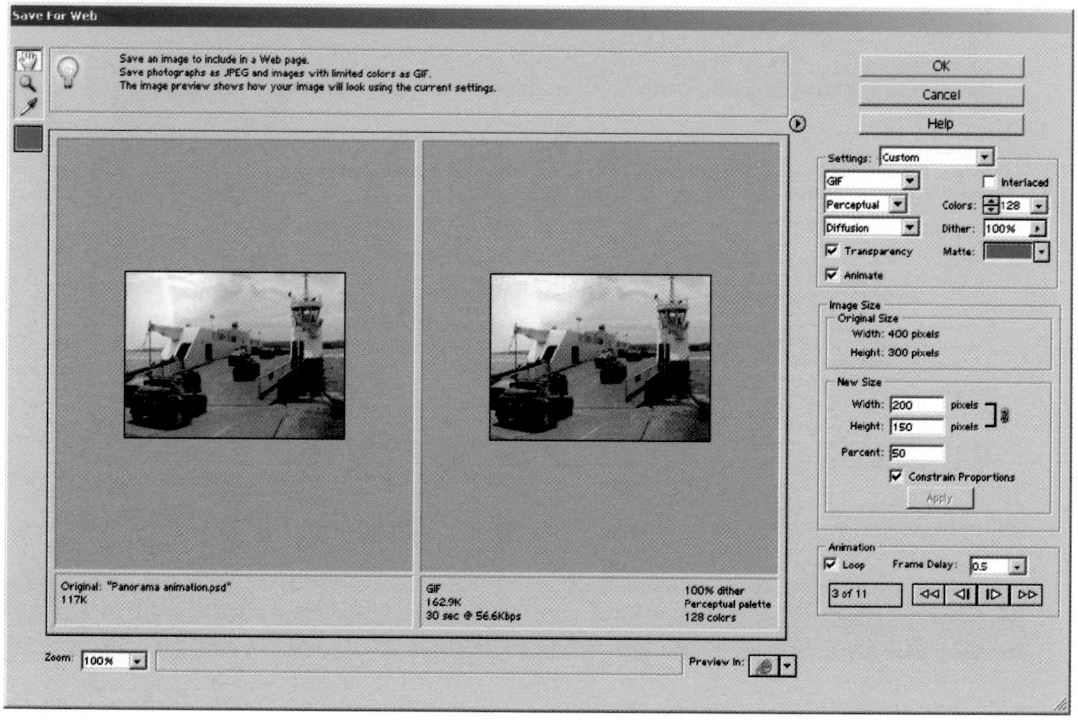

Figure 11.18: Save for Web settings

Tip: You could also have resized the image by selecting **Image**, **Resize**, **Image Size** from the **Menu bar**.

Save the animation as Panoramic animation for web.gif.

Viewing saved animations

To view the saved animated GIFs we need to open an Internet browser. You may have some other browser but we will look at Internet Explorer as it is the most widely used; the instructions will be similar for other browsers.

▶ Open Windows Explorer.

> **Tip:** You can open **Windows Explorer** by right-clicking on the **Start** button at the bottom-left of your screen, then selecting **Explore** from the shortcut menu that appears.

As some programs hijack the default opening of files the best and quickest way of opening animated GIFs is to drag and drop the file straight into the browser window; we'll do this now.

▶ Locate the file Panoramic animation for web.gif in Windows Explorer.

▶ Open Internet Explorer or another web browser.

▶ Making sure the browser window is visible, click the animation file in Windows Explorer, drag it over to the browser window then drop it.

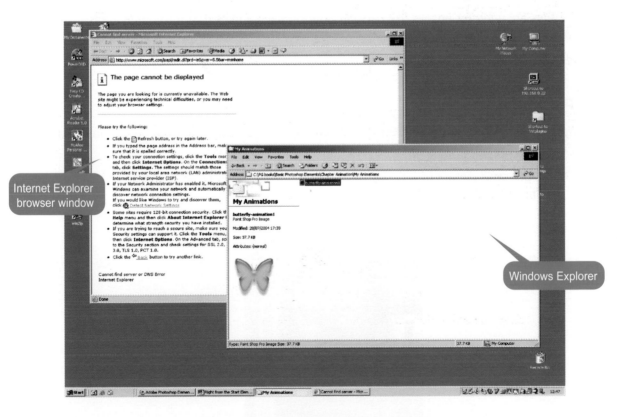

Figure 11.19: Drag and drop the GIF file

The animation should start in the browser window.

▶ When you're ready, close the animation by closing the browser window. Close Windows Explorer too if it is still open.

Optimising for the Web & Making a Slideshow

When you save images for the Web you need to make sure the file sizes are as small as possible to keep the download times short; nobody likes a slow website!

There are two main file formats available for Web pages: GIF and JPEG. Each of these formats compresses the file in a different way, and each format is best for a different type of image.

JPEGs (Joint Photographic Experts Group) are best for photographic images.

GIF files are good for images like cartoons and simple graphics that have large areas of similar colours.

We will try both formats now.

Saving a photo as a JPEG file

The photo of Bill is already a JPEG file, but this will work in the same way for a photo that is in a different format.

▶ Open your picture of Bill, switch off the frame layer you created and go to Layer, Flatten Image.

Figure 12.1: The picture of Bill you edited

Tip: If you don't have your picture of Bill to hand, any photo will do. You can always download the picture from **www.payne-gallway.co.uk/elements**.

○ From the File menu select Save for Web.

Most people who log onto the web have screen resolutions of 1024 pixels wide and 768 pixels high. So if our picture is 600 pixels wide and 400 pixels high it will take up over half the screen.

Apply ─○ Change the height of the image to 400 pixels then click Apply.

○ In Figure 12.2 you will see a close-up of the Save for Web window. Copy the settings, but have a play before clicking OK.

○ Set the Quality to 34. Try moving it to different values between 1 and 100, checking the difference in the proofing window on the right. When you start to see the image breaking up you have gone too far.

Progressive refers to the way the file downloads. With **Progressive** selected it will show the image in a very low resolution which gets higher as the file downloads. This increases the file size and does not work on some web browsers.
You can't use the **Optimised** function with the **Progressive** box selected.

Figure 12.2: Settings in the Save for Web window

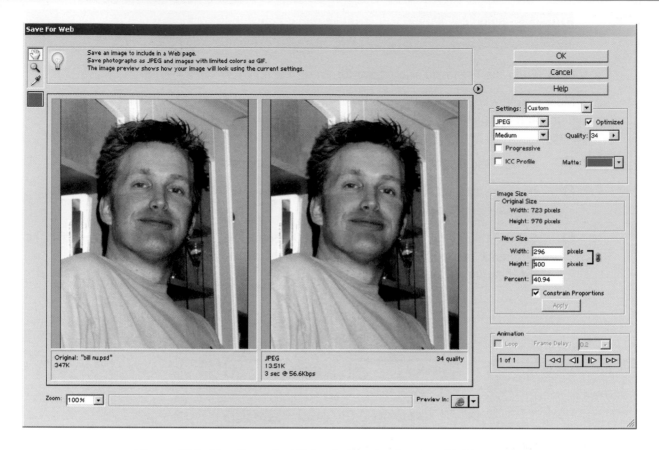

Figure 12.3: The Save for Web window – adjusting JPEG settings

Tip: Remember you can use the **Clone Stamp Tool** to touch-up your photos after you scan or download them.

- Click OK.

- Save the image as Bill-web-ready.jpg, then close it.

Saving a cartoon as a GIF file

Finally, we'll look at transforming a simple graphic to a GIF file suitable for the Web. By making it a GIF file, the file size will be much smaller.

▶ Let's load up the vector image Surprised bunny.psd. If you don't have yours to hand, download it from the Payne-Gallway website www.payne-gallway.co.uk/elements.

Figure 12.4: Surprised bunny.psd

▶ Select File, Save for Web from the Menu bar.

▶ Copy the settings in Figure 12.5. Notice that when you change the format from JPG to GIF the available settings change.

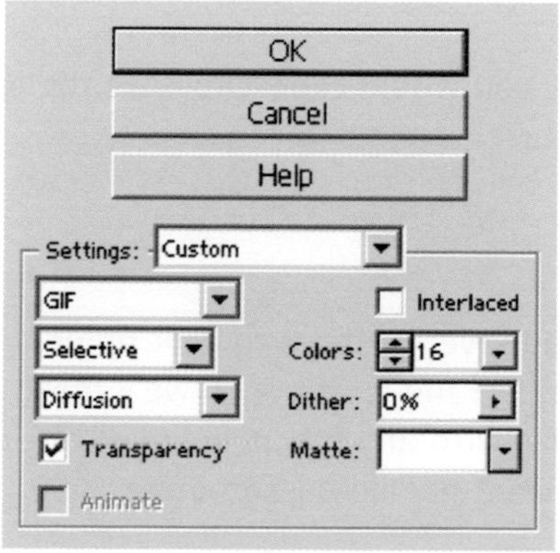

Play with the settings. Notice how the image is affected by the different settings, especially if you drop the number of colours. Look out for the edges of the image becoming pixelated.

Figure 12.5: GIF settings in the Save for Web window

Apply ▶ Change the height of the image in the Save for Web window to 600 pixels. Don't forget to click Apply.

▶ Click OK and save the optimized image as Surprised-bunny-web-ready.gif.

Typical file sizes for Web pages

At the bottom of the Save for Web window are the file sizes before and after optimisation for a download time at 28.8 Kbps; this is about the slowest home phone internet connection so this is a worst-case figure! You can right-click to choose a different download speed. There are also some zoom settings here.

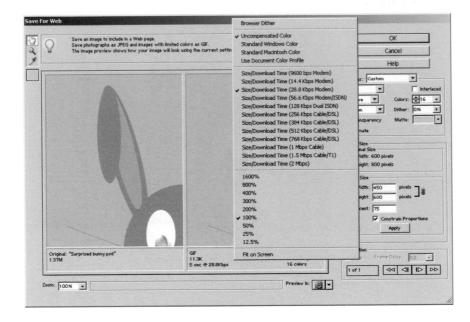

Figure 12.6: The file size, zoom and download settings in the Save for Web window

Below is a rough guide for image sizes on the Web:

2K: a small file (something like an icon or button for web site)

30k: a medium-sized file

125k: a large picture file – you would expect to have the option of whether or not to download it on a website

Transparent GIF

You will find that when you save for the web your original file stays open and unchanged. Whilst the Surprised bunny.psd file is still open we'll make it into an icon with a transparent background. You can do this with any file including layered files and text. You just need to make sure the image you want has no background.

We are going to save the bunny cartoon onto a transparent background.

◉   Select Layer, Flatten Image from the Menu bar.

◉   Click the Magic Eraser Tool and set the tolerance to 32 and opacity to 100%. Click the grey background behind the bunny.

The grey background is erased.

You will see a checker pattern behind the image to show there is no background

Figure 12.7: Transparent GIF

◉   Select File, Save for Web. Copy the settings in Figure 12.8; make sure the Transparency option is selected.

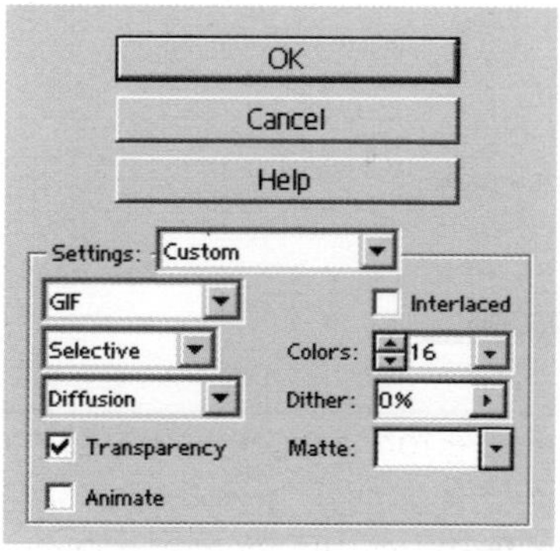

Figure 12.8: Transparent GIF settings in the Save for Web window

Apply ─◉   Change the image size in the Save for Web window to 100 pixels high, then click Apply.

◉   Click OK. Save the image as Surprised bunny icon.gif.

This is now ready to be pasted onto a web page!

Making a slideshow

A great way of showing off your photo retouching and pictures is by making a PDF slideshow of them. You will be able to view it in Adobe Acrobat Reader (it is free on the Photoshop Elements CD or downloadable free from the Adobe web site www.adobe.co.uk).

 Select File, Automation Tools, PDF Slideshow from the Menu bar.

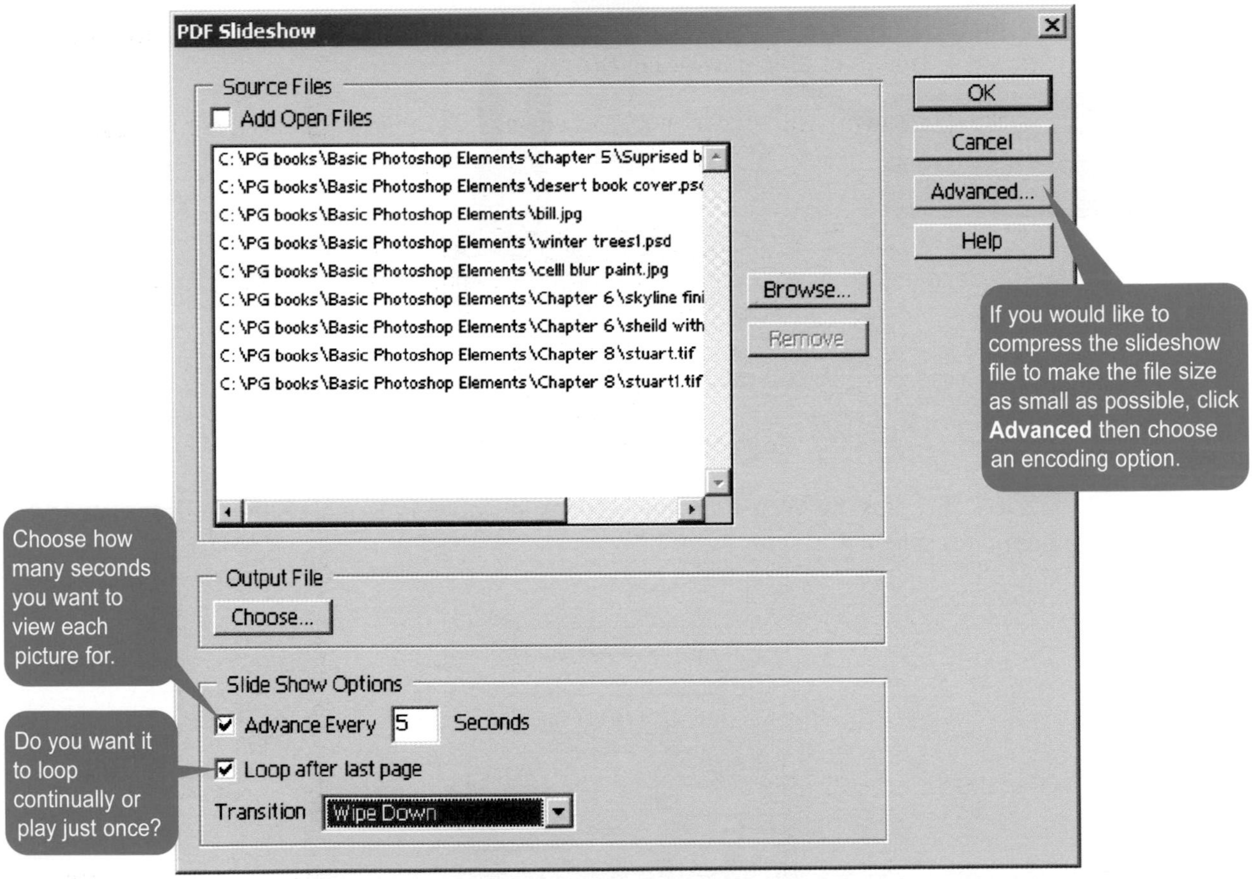

Figure 12.9: PDF Slide show options

Selecting files for the slideshow

`Browse...` ▶ First click the Browse button and navigate to the files you would like to use. If they are in a single folder you can hold down Shift and click them all to select them.

`Remove` ▶ If you want to remove a file, click it in the list and then click the Remove button. The images will display in the order they appear in this list; to change the order of the list, click and drag the files into a new position.

You will need to choose a place for Elements to save the PDF slideshow.

▶ Under Output File click Choose then find where you want to save the file.

▶ In the Transition drop-down list you can select the way your images appear, for example they can fade in or drop down from the top.

▶ Click OK. Elements will take a minute to compile all the images. You'll get a message to say the slideshow was successful; click OK again.

Figure 12.10: Successful Slideshow window

Tip: When the slideshow is finished, press the **Escape** key to minimize the Acrobat window.

Running the slideshow!

▶ Double-click the PDF file in Windows Explorer and Acrobat will open and run your slideshow!

Tip: You can save any image in a **PDF** format; simply select **File**, **Save As** from the menu. Enter a file name then select **Photoshop PDF** from the **Format** drop-down menu.

Figure 12.11: The PDF slideshow running in Arobat Reader

How professional! You can use this slideshow to show people a portfolio of your work.

Index